David MacRitchie

Fians Fairies and Picts

David MacRitchie

Fians Fairies and Picts

ISBN/EAN: 9783741196621

Manufactured in Europe, USA, Canada, Australia, Japa

Cover: Foto ©Thomas Meinert / pixelio.de

Manufactured and distributed by brebook publishing software
(www.brebook.com)

David MacRitchie

Fians Fairies and Picts

PLATE I.

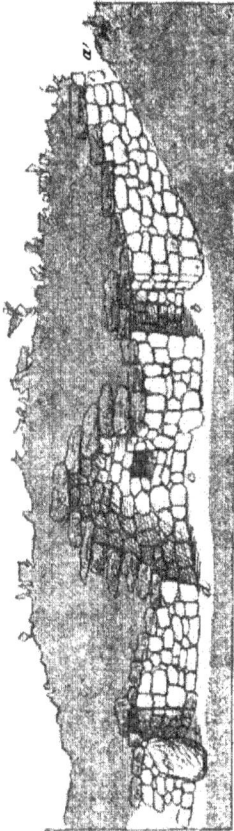

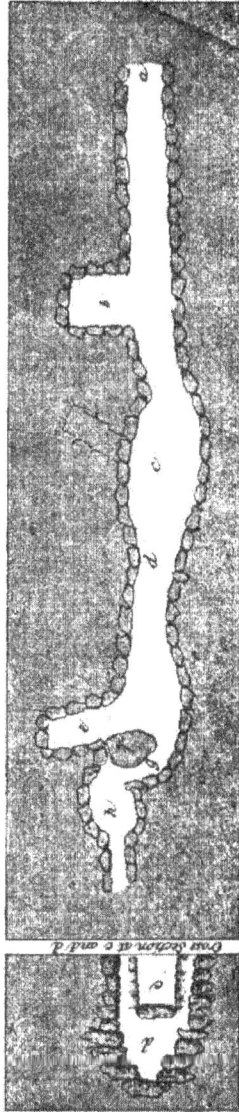

SECTIONAL VIEW AND GROUND PLAN OF UNDERGROUND GALLERY, CALLED *UAMH SGALABHAD*, NEAR MOL A DEAS, HUISHNISH, ISLAND OF SOUTH UIST.

Frontispiece.

FIANS, FAIRIES

AND

PICTS

BY

DAVID MacRITCHIE

AUTHOR OF

"THE TESTIMONY OF TRADITION"

> "Sometimes . . . . it seems that the stones are really speaking—speaking of the old things, of the time when the strange fishes and animals lived that are turned into stone now, and the lakes were here; and then of the time when the little Bushmen lived here, so small and so ugly, and used to sleep in the wild dog holes, and in the 'sloots,' and eat snakes, and shoot the bucks with their poisoned arrows. . . . . Now the Boers have shot them all, so that we never see a little yellow face peeping out among the stones. . . . . And the wild bucks have gone, and those days, and we are here."—WALDO, in *The Story of an African Farm.*

WITH ILLUSTRATIONS

LONDON

KEGAN PAUL, TRENCH, TRÜBNER & CO., L^{TD.}

PATERNOSTER HOUSE, CHARING CROSS ROAD

1893

INTRODUCTION.

THE following treatise is to some extent a re-statement and partly an amplification of a theory I have elsewhere advanced.[1] But as that theory, although it has been advocated by several writers, especially during the past half-century, is not familiar to everybody, some remarks of an explanatory nature are necessary. And if this explanation assumes a narrative form, not without a tinge of autobiography, it is because this seems the most convenient way of stating the case.

It is now a dozen years or thereabouts since I first read the "Popular Tales of the West Highlands," by Mr. J. F. Campbell, otherwise known by his courtesy-title of "Campbell of Islay." Mr. Campbell was, as many people know, a Highland gentleman of good family, who devoted much of his time to collecting and studying the oral traditions of his own district and of many lands. His equipment as a student of West Highland folklore was unique. He had the necessary

---

[1] *The Testimony of Tradition.* Kegan Paul, Trench, Trübner & Co., London, 1890.

knowledge of Gaelic, the hereditary connection with the district which made him at home with the poorest peasant, and the sympathetic nature which proved a master-key in opening the storehouse of inherited belief. It is not likely that another Campbell of Islay will arise, and, indeed, in these days of decaying tradition, he would be born too late.

In reading his book, then, for the first time, what impressed me more than anything else in his pages were statements such as the following :—

"The ancient Gauls wore helmets which represented beasts. The enchanted king's sons, when they come home to their dwellings, put off *cochal* [a Gaelic word signifying], the husk, and become men; and when they go out they resume the *cochal*, and become animals of various kinds. May this not mean that they put on their armour? They marry a plurality of wives in many stories. In short, the enchanted warriors are, as I verily believe, nothing but real men, and their manners real manners, seen through a haze of centuries. . . . . . I do not mean that the tales date from any particular period, but that traces of all periods may be found in them— that various actors have played the same parts time out of mind, and that their manners and customs are all mixed together, and truly, though confusedly, represented—that giants and fairies and enchanted princes were men . . . . that tales are but garbled popular history, of a long journey through forests and wilds, inhabited by savages and wild beasts; of events that occurred on the way from east to west, in the year of grace, once upon a time" (I. cxv.–cxvi.). "The

Highland giants were not so big but that their conquerors wore their clothes; they were not so strong that men could not beat them, even by wrestling. They were not quite savages ; for though some lived in caves, others had houses and cattle and hoards of spoil " (I. xcix.). " And though I do not myself believe that fairies *are* . . . . I believe there once was a small race of people in these islands, who are remembered as fairies, for the fairy belief is not confined to the Highlanders of Scotland " (I. c.) " This class of stories is so widely spread, so matter-of-fact, hangs so well together, and is so implicitly believed all over the United Kingdom, that I am persuaded of the former existence of a race of men in these islands who were smaller in stature than the Celts ; who used stone arrows, lived in conical mounds like the Lapps, knew some mechanical arts, pilfered goods and stole children; and were perhaps cotemporary with some species of wild cattle and horses and great auks, which frequented marshy ground, and are now remembered as water-bulls and water - horses, and boobries, and such like impossible creatures " (IV. 344).

And much more to the same effect,[1] with which it is unnecessary to trouble the reader. Now, all this was quite new to me. If I had ever given a second thought to the so-called " supernatural " beings of tradition, it was only to dismiss them, in the conventional manner as creatures of the imagination. But these ideas of Mr. Campbell's were decidedly interest-

---

[1] Such as at pp. ci.–cix. of Vol. I., and pp. 46, 101, and 275 of Vol. II.

ing, and deserving of consideration. It was obvious
that tradition, especially where there had been an
intermixture of races, could not preserve one clear,
unblemished record of the past ; and this he fully
recognised. But it seemed equally obvious that the
"matter-of-fact" element to which he refers could not
have owed its origin to myth or fancy. The question
being fascinating, there was therefore no alternative but
to make further inquiry. And the more it was con-
sidered, the more did his theory proclaim its reasonable-
ness. He suggests, for example, that certain "fairy
herds " in Sutherlandshire were probably reindeer, that
the "fairies" who milked those reindeer were probably
of the same race as Lapps, and that not unlikely they
were the people historically known as Picts. The
fact that Picts once occupied northern Scotland formed
no obstacle to his theory. And when I learned that
the reindeer was hunted in that part of Scotland as
recently as the twelfth century, that remains of reindeer
horns are still to be found in the counties of Suther-
land, Ross, and Caithness, sometimes in the very
structures ascribed to the Picts, then I perceived this
to be a theory which, to quote his words, "hung well
together." Further, the actual Lapps are a small-
statured race, the fairies also were so described, and
this, too, I found to be the traditional idea regarding
the Picts. Here the identification was closer still.

Then came the consideration: The fairies lived in hollow hillocks and under the ground: what kind of dwellings are the Picts supposed to have occupied? The answer to this question still further strengthened Mr. Campbell's conjecture. There yet exist numerous underground structures and artificial mounds whose interior shows them to have been dwelling-places; and these are in some places known as "fairy halls" and in others as "Picts' houses." (Illustrations of these are shown in the present volume, and are specially referred to in the annexed paper.)

The examination, therefore, of this interesting theory not only helped greatly to bear out its probable correctness, but it further began to appear that by following this method of ·inquiry new lights might be thrown upon history—perhaps upon very remote history. It was clear that the question was not a simple one. All tradition is obscured by the darkness of time, and genuine fact is mixed up with ideas which belong to the world of religion and of myth. Even in Mr. Campbell's own statements there were seeming contradictions. These, however, it is not my present purpose to discuss; since they do not vitally affect his main contention.

The Lapp-Dwarf parallel was gone into very fully by Professor Nilsson in his *Primitive Inhabitants of Scandinavia*, written twenty years before the " West

Highland Tales." Not that he, either, was the
originator of that theory, for it is frequently referred to
by Sir Walter Scott, who accepted it himself.[1] "In
fact," he says, "there seems reason to conclude that
these *duergar* [in English, *dwarfs*] were originally
nothing else than the diminutive natives of the
Lappish, Lettish and Finnish nations, who, flying
before the conquering weapons of the Asae, sought the
most retired regions of the north, and there endeavoured
to hide themselves from their eastern invaders." Scott,
again, refers us back to Einar Gudmund, an Icelandic
writer of the second half of the sixteenth century, whom
I would cite as the earliest "Euhemerus" of northern
lands, were it not for the fact that he is obviously much
more than a theorist, and is beyond all doubt speaking
of an actual race, as may be seen from an incident
which he relates.

But, although the popular memory may retain for
many centuries the impress of historical facts, these
become inevitably blurred and modified by the lapse
of time and the ignorance of the very people who
preserve the tradition. As an illustration of this, I
may cite the instance of the dwarfs of Yesso, referred
to in the following pages. These people still survived

---

[1] Scott, however, had only imperfectly grasped this idea. In
numerous passages he inconsistently refers to "the little people"
as purely the creatures of imagination.

as a separate community until the first half of the seventeenth century, if not later. They occupied semi-subterranean or "pit" dwellings, and are said to have been under four feet in height. But, although the modern inhabitants of that island still describe them, on the whole, in these terms, a new belief regarding them has recently sprouted up in one corner. The Aïno word signifying "pit-dweller" is also not unlike the word for a burdock leaf. It was known that those dwarfs were little people. Obviously, then, their name must have meant "people living under burdock leaves" (instead of "in pits"). And so, to some of the modern natives of Yesso, those historical dwarfs of the seventeenth century "were so small that if caught in a shower of rain or attacked by an enemy, they would stand beneath a burdock leaf for shelter, or flee thither to hide."[1]

In that instance, we see before our eyes the whole process by which a real race has been transformed into an unreal impossibility, within a period of two centuries or so. Had the extinction (or modification by intermarriage or by the processes of evolution) of those

---

[1] A description of those dwarfs, obtained from Japanese records and pictures, may be seen in my monograph on "The Aïnos" (Supplement to Vol. IV. of the *Internationales Archiv für Ethnographie*, Leiden, 1892). Kegan Paul, Trench, Trübner & Co., London.

Yesso dwarfs taken place a thousand years earlier, the difficulty of identifying them would have been greatly increased. After a race has once disappeared from sight, the popular terms describing it must become more vague and confused with every century. Thus, in a certain traditional Scotch story there is mention of a number of "little black creatures with spades." The description is delightfully comprehensive. It would be quite applicable to a gang of Andaman coolies. On the other hand, if we exclude the "spades," it might be applied to any "little black creatures"—say a colony of tadpoles or of black-beetles. So that, when a poet or an artist gets hold of a tradition which has reached this stage of uncertainty, he may give the reins to his fancy, so long as he portrays some kind—any kind—of "little black creatures." [1]

Before parting altogether from the Yesso dwarfs, notice may be taken of a folk-tale containing an

[1] Similarly, the "little Bushmen" referred to by Miss Olive Schreiner's *Waldo* (as quoted by me on the title-page) would be remembered with as much uncertainty a century hence if the modern population of South Africa had nothing but tradition to depend upon. (It may be explained, in case of misapprehension on the part of any too-literal reader, that that quotation is not supposed to prove that the earth-dwellers of the Hebrides were small and ugly, with "little yellow faces," any more than it proves the reindeer of Scotland to have been identical with the wild buck of South Africa. But the cases are analogous, and the quotation seems *à propos*.)

incident which obviously derives its existence from
them, or from a branch of their race. In Mr. Andrew
Lang's "Green Fairy Book" there is introduced a
certain Chinese "Story of Hok Lee and the Dwarfs."
It appears to be also current in Japan, to judge from a
reviewer's remark, that "the clever artist who has
illustrated the book must have known the Japanese
story, for he gets some of his ideas from the Japanese
picture-maker." In the story of Hok Lee the dwarfs
are represented as living in subterranean dwellings, and
in the picture they are portrayed as half-naked, with
(for the most part) shaggy beards and eyebrows, and
bald heads. It is wonderfully near the truth. The
baldness is one of the most striking characteristics of
those actual dwarfs, and is caused by a certain skin-
disease, induced by their dirty habits, from which a
great number of them suffer, or did suffer. The
shaggy beards and eyebrows are equally characteristic
of the race ; and their custom of occupying half-under-
ground dwellings has given them the name by which
they are remembered in Japan at the present day.
The exact scene of the story is a matter of minor
importance. Those people appear to have been known
to the Chinese for at least twelve centuries, and to the
Japanese for a much longer period. Thus, it was
quite unnecessary for any novelist in China or Japan to
invent such people, since they already existed. As for

the details of that particular story, or of any other of the kind, it is not to be supposed that a belief in its historical basis necessarily implies an acceptance of every statement contained in it. On this principle, one would be bound to accept the truth of every " snake-story," for the simple reason that one believed in the existence of snakes. Still, it is possible, and perhaps not improbable, that tales which preserve the memory of those people, may also be fairly accurate in many of the statements made regarding them. The reason, however, of introducing this particular story is to show that the Chinese or Japanese romancer did not require to *create* a race of bald-headed, shaggy, half-wild dwarfs, seeing that that had already been done for him by the Creator.

Those to whom this question is a new one will now see what is the point of view of the realist or euhemerist with regard to such traditions. He sees here and there in the past, through much intervening mist, something that looks like a real object, and he tries to define its outlines. He has no intention of denying, as some have vainly imagined, that there *is* an intervening mist. Nor, it seems necessary to explain, does he assume that wherever there is a mist there must be some tangible object behind it. For example, he does not believe that Boreas, or Zephyrus, or Jack Frost were ever anything but personifications of certain natural forces.

Various other considerations have also to be borne in mind ; not the least important of which is the fact that the very people who have preserved these traditional beliefs have done much to obscure them, owing to their want of education. Scott tells a story of a Scotch peasant who, discovering a company of gaily-dressed puppets standing in a thicket, where they had been concealed by a travelling showman, at once concluded that they were "fairies." He had inherited the belief that fairies were "little people" who frequented just such places as this ; consequently, he decided these were fairies. This fact was elicited in court, where the countryman had to appear as a witness. From that time onward his mind ought to have been disabused of his hasty belief. But a man so stupid as to assume that a showman's marionettes were anything else than lifeless dolls, might continue for the rest of his life to recount his marvellous meeting with "the fairies." Similarly, to a tipsy man returning homeward from market, many common and every-day objects take on a weird and superhuman aspect, due to no other spirits than those he has consumed. From this cause, a large number of odd stories (such as one told by Mr. William Black of a tipsy Hebridean) has doubtless arisen. Further, the belief in the existence of "supernatural" beings has been much utilised by rustic humourists, and no doubt also by smugglers and

other night-birds, in comparatively recent times. The
prolonged absence of a husband, or it may be of a
wife, could be explained by some wild legend of
having been "stolen by the fairies," when a more
frank avowal dared not be offered. And although
"strange tales were told" regarding the paternity of
"Brian," in *The Lady of the Lake*, and although Scott
adheres to those legends in his poem, he does not fail
to point out in his appended *Note* that the story could
be explained in a much more rational manner. There
have been many "Brians."

To give this subject the special attention which it
deserves would, however, swell these introductory notes
to an intolerable size; and, indeed, their purpose is
rather to show what the euhemeristic theory is than
what it is not; that is to say, the euhemeristic theory
as applied to the traditions relating to dwarf races.

In the work to which I have referred, the opinions
enunciated by Professor Nilsson and Mr. J. F.
Campbell, together with other developments which
suggested themselves to me, were duly set forth, and
were received, as was to be expected, with every form
of comment, from complete approval to entire dissent.
Among the adverse criticisms, some arose from a misapprehension of the case, while others were due to
the critic's imperfect acquaintance with the subject he
professed to discuss. But besides these, there were of

course the legitimate objections which can always be urged in matters of a debateable character, where there is no positive evidence on either side. With regard to such I can at least echo the words of one of the most eminent and most courteous of my opponents, M. Charles Ploix, and say for euhemerism what he says for naturalism :—" Tant que la théorie sur laquelle il s'appuie n'aura pas été démontrée fausse par des arguments décisifs, et surtout tant qu'elle n'aura pas été remplacée par une hypothèse plus certaine, il pourra continuer à s'affirmer."[1]

It ought to be mentioned that the following paper was written for the Folk-Lore Society, at one of whose meetings (in February 1892) it was subsequently read. As, however, the Council of that Society ultimately decided that the paper was unsuited for publication in a journal devoted to the study of folk-lore, it now appears in a separate form. One advantage to be derived from this is that the illustrations which accompanied the lecture, and which are of much importance in enabling one to understand the argument, can also be reproduced at the same time. It may be added that, while the theme is capable of much amplification,[2] I have preferred to print the paper

---

[1] *Le Surnaturel dans les Contes Populaires*, Paris, 1891, p. iv.

[2] Some portions of it I have already amplified : in a pamphlet entitled "The Underground Life," Edinburgh, 1892 (privately

B

as it was written for the occasion referred to. It states, concisely enough, the leading points of the argument.

To those who are interested in the "realistic" interpretation of such traditions, I beg to recommend for reference the following works :—First and foremost, there is "The Anatomy of a Pygmie," by Dr. Edward Tyson (London, 1699), a book full of suggestive notices. This author has undoubtedly reached the "bed-rock" of the question ; but, owing to his era and mental environment, he has not realised that his argument is useless without a consideration of the various stratifications above the "bed-rock." Belonging to the same century is the chapter "Of Pigmies" in Sir Thomas Browne's "Vulgar Errors," wherein he makes several very interesting statements, although he argues from the opposite side. Scattered throughout the writings of Sir Walter Scott, both poetry and prose, there are also many references bearing upon this question, from the realistic point of view. In addition to these, there is his well-known treatise "On the Fairies of Popular Superstition," prefaced to "The Tale of Tamlane," wherein he states that "the most distinct account of the duergar [*i.e.* dwergs, or dwarfs], or elves, and their attributes, is to be found in a preface of

printed); in a paper on "Subterranean Dwellings," contributed to *The Antiquary* (London : Elliot Stock) of August 1892 ; and at pp. 52–58 of "The Aïnos," previously quoted.

Torfæus to the history of Hrolf Kraka [Copenhagen, 1715], who cites a dissertation by Einar Gudmund, a learned native of Iceland. 'I am firmly of opinion,' says the Icelander, 'that these beings are creatures of God, consisting, like human beings,' of a body and rational soul; that they are of different sexes, and capable of producing children, and subject to all human affections, as sleeping and waking, laughing and crying, poverty and wealth; and that they possess cattle and other effects, and are obnoxious to death, like other mortals.' He proceeds to state that the females of this race are capable of procreating with mankind;' and gives an account of one who bore a child to an inhabitant of Iceland, for whom she claimed the privilege of baptism; depositing the infant for that purpose at the gate of the churchyard, together with a goblet of gold as an offering."² Scott further cites from Jessen's *De Lapponibus* similar matter-of-fact details obtained on this subject from the Lapps; who, on their own showing, are inferentially the half-bred descendants of dwarfs.

---

¹ By "mankind" need only be understood the race to which Einar Gudmund belonged. It is well known that many races apply the term "men" to themselves alone. At the same time, Gudmund's words may denote a very marked difference in the two types.

² Scott again quotes this story, in fuller detail, in the Appendix to *The Lady of the Lake*, Note 3 C.

"That some of the myths of giants and dwarfs are connected with traditions of real indigenous or hostile tribes is settled beyond question by the evidence brought forward by Grimm, Nilsson, and Hanusch," observes Dr. E. B. Tylor.[1] And although that eminent anthropologist sees a different meaning in many kindred traditions, yet his observations, and the great mass of references which he gives in connection with this single detail, are of much interest to euhemerists pure and simple. The late Sir Daniel Wilson's "Caliban"[2] teems with the realistic doctrine, and so also does a work of (in my opinion) less equal merit, "The Pedigree of the Devil,"[3] by Mr. Frederic T. Hall. In Mr. R. G. Haliburton's "Dwarfs of Mount Atlas: with notes as to Dwarfs and Dwarf Worship,"[4] and also in his "Further Notes"[5] on that subject, the same idea is prominent. All of these writers, with the exception of Sir Thomas Browne (and excluding Dr. Tylor in so far as regards some of his deductions), refer practically, though in varying degrees, to the question discussed by Tyson; and in this respect I must also cite my recent work on "The

[1] "Primitive Culture," vol. i. p. 385 (3rd edition).
[2] London, Macmillan and Co., 1873.
[3] London, Trübner and Co., 1883.
[4] London, David Nutt, 1891.
[5] Asiatic Quarterly Review, July 1892.

Aïnos" (pp. 51–66). Of other writers who have not probed quite so deeply, and who possibly may not recognise the necessity for so doing, but who are realists nevertheless, the following may be mentioned : M. Paul Monceaux, who, in the *Revue Historique* of October 1891, deals with the African dwarfs of ancient and modern writers ;[1] Professor Henri van Elven, the main theme of whose forthcoming work, *Les Nains préhistoriques de l'Europe Occidentale,* formed the subject of a paper recently read by him before the *Société d'Archéologie de Bruxelles ;* and MM. Grandgagnage and De Reul, cited by Mr. C. Carter Blake, F.G.S., in connection with the *Nutons* of the Belgian bone-caves;[2] as also another writer of the Low Countries, Van den Bergh (" xxx. and 313 "), whom Mr. J. Dirks quotes at p. 15 of his *Heidens of Egyptiërs,* Utrecht, 1850. In Mr. W. G. Black's charming book on Heligoland,[3] one passage (p. 72) recognises that a certain Sylt tradition " is evidently one of those valuable legends which illuminate dark pages of history. It clearly bears

---

[1] For an exhaustive account of "The Pygmy Tribes of Africa," treated from the purely scientific and ethnological point of view see Dr. Henry Schlichter's articles in *The Scottish Geographical Magazine* of June and July 1892.

[2] *Memoirs* of the Anthropological Society of London, vol. iii. 1870, pp. 320, 321.

[3] Blackwood and Sons, 1888.

testimony to the same small race having inhabited Friesland in times which we trace in the caves of the Neolithic age, and of which the Esquimaux are the only survivors." For many of the kindred traditions in that locality, one cannot do better than refer to Mr. Christian Jensen's *Zwergsagen aus Nordfriesland,* contributed to the *Zeitschrift des Vereins für Volkskunde* (Berlin, Heft 4, 1892).

[The foregoing pages were all in type before the appearance of Vol. VIII. of the *Bibliothèque de Carabas,* which contains several criticisms by Mr. Andrew Lang on my "Testimony of Tradition" and "Underground Life." The already excessive length of this Introduction prevents me from now referring more particularly to these observations, as I should otherwise have done. In the meantime, however, I beg to refer Mr. Lang to the present work, and to ask him whether he thinks the statements there quoted substantiate his conception of the *Fir Sidhe* as a deathless people, occupying some region "unknown of earth."

An addition to the Bibliography of this subject is made in the above-named volume (p. 88). "In his *Scottish Scenery* (1803), Dr. Cririe suggests that the germ of the Fairy myth is the existence of dispossessed aboriginals dwelling in subterranean houses, in some places called Picts' houses, covered with artificial mounds. The lights seen near the mounds are lights actually carried by the mound-dwellers." Mr. Lang adds : " Dr. Cririe works out in some detail 'this marvellously absurd supposition,' as the *Quarterly Review* calls it (vol. lix. p. 280)."]

FIANS, FAIRIES AND PICTS.

THE general belief at the present day is that, of the three designations here classed together, only that of the Picts is really historical. The Fians are regarded as merely legendary—perhaps altogether mythical beings ; and the Fairies as absolutely unreal. On the other hand, there are those who believe that the three terms all relate to historical people, closely akin to each other, if not actually one people under three names.

To those unacquainted with the views of the realists, or euhemerists, it is necessary to explain that the popular definition of Fairies as "little people" is one which that school is quite ready to accept. But the conception of such "little people" as tiny beings of aërial and ethereal nature, able to fly on a bat's back, or to sip honey from the flowers "where the bee sucks,"

is regarded by the realists as simply the out-
come of the imagination, working upon a basis
of fact. An illustration of this position may be
seen in the Far East. There is a tradition among
the Aïnos of Northern Japan that they were preceded by a race of "little people," only a few
inches in height, whose pit-dwellings they still
point out. But the pottery and the skeletons
associated with these habitations show that not
only were their occupants of a stature to be
measured by feet rather than by inches, but also
that, by reason of a certain anatomical peculiarity
common to both, the traditional dwarfs were very
clearly the ancestors of the Aïnos—a race which,
though now blended, was once most distinctly a
race of dwarfs, if one is to believe the earliest
Japanese pictures of them. Similarly, the dwarfs
of European tradition are believed to have had
as real an origin as the little people of Aïno
legend, at any rate by those who hold the realistic
theory.

Any attempt to reconcile the pygmies of the
classic writers with actual dwarfs of flesh and
blood is outside my province. Moreover, this

has been admirably, and, as it seems to me, successfully done quite recently by M. Paul Monceaux, in an article in the *Revue Historique*,[1] wherein he compares the traditional and historical descriptions with the statements of modern travellers, and draws the inference that the pygmies of the Greek and Roman writers, sculptors and painters, are all derived from actual dwarfs seen by their forefathers in Africa and India. (Still less doubt is there with regard to the dwarfs in Ancient Egyptian paintings.) And whereas Strabo is, says M. Monceaux, the only writer of antiquity who questions the existence of the dwarfs, all the others are on the side of Aristotle, who says—"This is no fable; there really exists in that region (the sources of the Nile), as people relate, a race of little men, who have small horses and who live in holes." And these little men were of course the ancestors of Schweinfurth's and Stanley's dwarfs.

But although M. Monceaux confines his identification to equatorial Africa and to India, he does

---

[1] "*La légende des Pygmées et les nains de l'Afrique equatoriale*": *Rev. Hist.* t. 47, I. (Sept.-Oct. 1891), pp. 1-64.

not omit to state that Pliny and other writers
speak of dwarf tribes in other localities, and
among these are "the vague regions of the north,
designated by the name of Thule." This area,
vague enough certainly, is the territory with which
Fians and Picts are both associated; as, also, of
course, the Fairies of North European tradition.

The attributes with which the "little people"
of North Europe are accredited cannot be given
in detail here. It is enough to note that they
were believed to live in houses wholly or partly
underground, the latter kind being described as
"hollow" mounds, or hills; that when people of
taller race entered such subterranean dwellings
(as occasionally they did) they found the domestic
utensils of the dwarfs were of the kind labelled
"pre-historic" in our antiquarian museums; that
the copper vessels which dwarf women sometimes
left behind them when discovered surreptitiously
milking the cows of their neighbours, were likewise
of an antique form; further, that they helped themselves to the beef and mutton of their neighbours,
after having shot the animals with flint-headed
arrows; that melodies peculiar to them are still

sung by the peasants of certain localities ; that words used by them are still employed by children in their games; and that many families in many districts are believed to have inherited some of their blood.[1] Of this intercourse between the taller races and the dwarfs, there are many records in old traditions. In the days of King Arthur, when, as Chaucer tells us, the land was "ful-filled of faërie," the knights errant had usually a dwarf as attendant. One of King Arthur's own knights was a Fairy.[2] According to Highland tradition, every high-caste family of pure Gaelic descent had an attendant dwarf. These examples show the "little people " in a not unfriendly light. But many other stories speak of them as "malignant" foes, and as dreaded oppressors. Of which the rational explanation is that these various tales relate to various localities and epochs.

[1] For some of these references see Dr. Hibbert's " Description of the Shetland Islands," Edinburgh, 1822, pp. 444–451. See also Mrs. J. E. Saxby's " Folk-Lore from Unst, Shetland " (in *Leisure Hour* of 1880) ; Mr. W. G. Black's " Heligoland", 1888, chap. iv. ; and "The Fians," London, 1891, pp. 2–3.

[2] Gwynn the son of Nudd : for whom see Lady C. Guest's " Mabinogion," pp. 223, 263–5, and 501–2.

The connection visible between Fians and
Fairies, between Fians and Picts, and between
Picts and Fairies, may now briefly be stated.

The earliest known association of the first two
classes occurs in an Irish manuscript of the
eleventh or twelfth century,[1] wherein it is stated
that when the ninth-century Danes overran and
plundered Ireland, there was nothing "in con-
cealment under ground in Erinn, or in the
various secret places belonging to Fians or
to Fairies" that they did not discover and
appropriate. This statement receives strong
confirmation from a Scandinavian record, the
Landnáma-bok, which says[2] that, in or about the
year 870, a well-known Norse chief named Leif

"went on warfare in the west. He made war in Ireland, and
there found a large underground house; he went down into it,
and it was dark until light shone from a sword in the hand of
a man. Leif killed the man, and took the sword and much
property. . . . . He made war widely in Ireland, and got
much property. He took ten thralls."

Although the Scandinavian record does not

---

[1] "The War of the Gaedhil with the Gaill," edited by J. H. Todd,
D.D., London, 1867, pp. 114-115.

[2] I. cc. 4-6 (this reference and the passage is quoted from Du
Chaillu's "Viking Age," vol. ii. p. 516).

speak of the owner of the earth-house as either a " Fian " or a " Fairy," it is quite evident that this is an example of the plundering referred to in the Irish chronicle, and that the Gaels of Ireland seven or eight centuries ago, if not a thousand years ago, regarded the underground people as indifferently Fians and Fairies.[1]

Many other associations of Fians with Fairies are to be seen. In one of the old traditional ballads regarding the Fians, they are described as feasting with Fairies in one of their "hollow " mounds.[2] A Sutherlandshire story relates the adventures of the son of a Fairy woman, who took service with Ossian, the king of the Fians.[3] One of the Fians (Caoilte) had a Fairy sweetheart.[4] Another of them (Oscar) has an interview with a washerwoman who is a Fairy.[5] A Fenian story recounts how one day the Fians were working in the harvest-field, in the Argyleshire island of Tiree, and on that occasion they

---

[1] " *Fianaibh ag Sithcuiraibh.*"
[2] " *Dan an Fhir Shicair*"; *Leabhar na Feinne*, pp. 94–95.
[3] *Folk-Lore Journal*, vol. vi. 1888, pp. 173–178.
[4] *The Fians*, 1891, p. 64.
[5] *Ibid.* p. 33.

had "left their weapons of war in the armoury
of the Fairy Hill of Caolas";[1] from which one
is to infer that the Fians made use of Fairy
dwellings.   In the same collection of tales we
are told[2] that one time when the Fians were
hunting in the Isle of Skye, they left their wives
in a dwelling which bore a title "applied to
dwellings of the Elfin race." It is further stated
that one popular belief in the Scottish Highlands is that the Fians are still lying in the
hill of Tomnahurich, near Inverness, and that
"others say they are lying in Glenorchy, Argyleshire."[3]   Now, both the Inverness-shire mound
and the mounds in Glenorchy are also popularly
regarded as the abodes of Fairies.[4]   The vitrified
fort on Knock-Farril, in Ross-shire, is said to

---

[1] *The Fians*, p. 172.   The Fairy Hill referred to is "a hillock,
in which there is to be seen a small hollow called the armoury"
(p. 174).

[2] *Ibid.* pp. 12–13, 166, &c.

[3] *Ibid.* pp. 3–4.   Glenorchy is said to have teemed with Fenian
traditions about the early part of this century (*Proceedings* of Soc.
of Antiq. of Scotland, vol. vii. pp. 237–240).

[4] See my *Testimony of Tradition*, London, 1890, pp. 146–8; and
Pennant's "Second Tour in Scotland" (Pinkerton's *Voyages*,
London, 1809, vol. iii. p. 368).

have been one of Fin McCoul's castles ;[1] and
Knock-Farril, or rather "a knoll opposite Knock-
Farril" is remembered as the abode of the Fairies
of that district.[2]   Glenshee, in Perthshire, is celebrated equally as a Fairy haunt and as a favourite
hunting-ground of the Fians. The Fians, indeed,
were said to have lived by deer-hunting, so much
so that Campbell of Islay suggests that their
name signifies "the deer men"; and the deer, it
is believed, "were a fairy race."[3]   The famous
hound of the famous leader of the Fians was "a
Fairy or Elfin dog." In short, the connection
between Fians and Fairies, recognised in the
Gaelic manuscript of eight or ten centuries ago,
is apparent throughout the traditions of the
Gaelic-speaking people.

But if the Fians were either identical with, or
closely akin to the Fairies, they must have been
"little people."   The belief that they were so
is supported by one traditional Fenian story.

---

[1] *Proceedings* of Society of Antiquaries of Scotland, vol. vii.
p. 294, *note.*

[2] See, for example, an article on "Scottish Customs and Folk
lore," in *The Glasgow Herald* of August 1, 1891.

[3] *The Fians*, pp. 78-80.

This is the well-known tale of the visit of Fin,
the famous chief of the Fians, to a country known
to him and his people as " The Land of the Big
Men." The story tells how Fin sailed from
Dublin Bay in his skin-boat, crossed the sea to
that country, and shortly after landing was cap-
tured and taken to the palace of the king, where
he was appointed court dwarf,[1] and remained for
a considerable time the attached and faithful
adherent of the king. The collector of this story
has assumed that it is purely imaginary. But
let it be contrasted with the following extract
from the *Heimskringla.* The period is the early
part of the eleventh century, and the scene
Norway : " There was a man from the Uplands
called Fin the Little, and some said of him that
he was of Finnish race. He was a remarkable
[? remarkably] little man, but so swift of foot
that no horse could overtake him. . . . . He had
long been in the service of King Hrorek, and
often employed in errands of trust. . . . . Now
when King Hrorek was set under guards on the

---

[1] *Scottish Celtic Review,* 1885, pp. 184–90 : *The Fians,* pp.
175–184.

journey Fin would often slip in among the men
of the guard, and followed, in general, with the
lads and serving-men; but as often as he could
he waited upon Hrorek, and entered into con-
versation with him."[1] And, like Fin the dwarf in
the Gaelic story, this little Fin rendered great
service to his king. Now, the *Heimskringla* Fin
is unquestionably a historical personage, and the
account of him was written by a twelfth century
historian. The Gaelic story was only obtained
in the Hebrides, and reduced to writing twenty-
three years ago. Although Fin of the Fians is
stated in Irish records to be the grandson of a
Finland woman,[2] and although the Scandinavian
and the Hebridean tales look very much like
two versions of one story, this cannot precisely
be the case, as the Fenian Fin is placed in an
earlier era than his namesake of Norway. A
dwarf king named Fin is also remembered in

[1] *The Heimskringla :* Dr. Rasmus B. Anderson's 2nd ed. (1889)
of Mr. Samuel Laing's translation from Snorre Sturlason : chap.
lxxxiii., *Of Little Fin.*

[2] *Leabhar na Feinne,* p. 34.

[SUBSEQUENT NOTE.—To be very accurate, one ought to say
that, in the pedigree referred to, Fin's grandfather (Trenmor) is
stated to have married a Finland woman.]

C

Frisian tradition ;[1] and that he and his race were
small men is pretty clearly proved by the fact
that when one of the earth-houses attributed to
him was opened some years ago, it was found to
contain the bones of a little man.[2] Both of these
dwarf Fins, Little Fin of Norway and Little
Fin of Denmark, are undoubtedly real; and
there seems no good reason to suppose that the
dwarf Fin of Hebridean tradition was not equally
real. Whether they were three separate people
is a problem. " Fin " appears to have been at
one time a not uncommon name, whatever its
etymology and that of "Fian" may be. At any
rate, there is nothing in history (which speaks of
a close intercourse between Scandinavia and
the British Isles, in former times), and nothing

[1] Mr. W. G. Black's *Heligoland*, 1888, chap. iv.

[2] With this Fin of Frisian tradition may be compared Fin, a
North-Frisian chief of the fifth century, mentioned in *Beowulf* and
The Gleeman's Tale, and whose death is recorded in *The Fight at
Finnsburh*.

[SUBSEQUENT NOTE.—A suitable companion to the dwarf Fin
of Frisian tradition is mentioned in Harald Hardradi's Saga :—
" Tuta, a Frisian, was with King Harald ; he was sent to him for
show, for he was short and stout, in every respect shaped like a
dwarf."—Quoted by Mr. Du Chaillu at p. 357 of vol. ii. of "The
Viking Age."]

in the ethnology of North-Western Europe, to make us regard as mythical the capture and enthralment of any one of these three "little Fins." If Fin of the Fians, therefore, was a typical Fian, they were little people.[1]

In regarding the Fians as a race of dwarfs, I do not overlook the fact that they are also spoken of as "giants." But to assume them to have been of gigantic stature is both totally at variance with the bulk of the evidence regarding them, and at variance with the fact that the word "giant" has very frequently been used to denote a savage, or a cave-dweller.[2] No more appropriate illustration

---

[1] In this connection it is worth noting that Sir Walter Scott, in referring to the aboriginal or servile clans in 1745, whom he describes as "half naked, *stinted in growth*, and miserable in aspect," includes among them the McCouls, Fin's alleged descendants, who "were a sort of Gibeonites, or hereditary servants to the Stewarts of Appin." (Waverley, ch. xliv.)

[2] For example, the late Rev. J. G. Campbell, Tiree, says of "the Great Tuairisgeul" that he was "a giant of the kind called *Samhanaich*—that is, one who lived in a cave by the sea-shore, the strongest and coarsest of any" (*Scottish Celtic Review*, p. 62). That this term was one of contempt, given by Gaelic-speaking people to those "giants" (and apparently based upon their malodorous characteristics), will be seen from Mr. Campbell's further observation (*op. cit.* pp. 140-141) :—" It is a common expression to say of any strong offensive smell, *mharbhadh e na Samhanaich,*

of this can be found than the local tradition that
a certain artificially hollowed rock in the island
of Hoy, Orkney, was the abode of "a giant and
his wife." Now, this same "giant" is also remembered as a "dwarf," and the largest cell in his
dwelling is only 5 feet 8 inches long. Similarly,

it would kill the giants who dwell in caves by the sea. *Samh* is a
strong oppressive smell." McAlpine defines *Samh* as a "bad
smell arising from a sick person, or a dirty hot place"; and he
further gives the definition "a savage" (quoting Mackenzie). The
word *Samhanach* itself is defined by McAlpine as "a savage," and
he cites the Islay saying :—"*chuireadh tu eagal air na samhanaich*," "you would frighten the very savages." From these
definitions it will be seen that a word translated "giant" by one is
rendered "savage" by another (though neither of these terms
expresses the literal meaning). Mr. J. G. Campbell also practically
regards it as signifying "cave-dweller," or perhaps a certain
special caste of cave-dwellers. With this may be compared
McAlpine's "*uamh, n. f.*, a cave, den; *n. m.*, a chief of savages,
terrible fellow . . . . . '*cha'n'eil ann ach uamh dhuine*,' 'he is
only a savage of a fellow.'" Islay has also another word to denote
a Hebridean savage. This is *ciuthach*, " pr. *kewach*, described in
the Long Island as naked wild men living in caves " (J. F. Campbell, Tales, iii. 55, *n*.). One of these "kewachs" figures in the
story of Diarmaid and Grainne, and one version says that he
"came in from the western ocean in a coracle with two oars
(*curachan*)" (*The Fians*, p. 54). (His name assumes various
shapes—*e.g.*, Ciofach Mac a Ghoill, Ciuthach Mac an Doill,
Ceudach Mac Righ nan Collach.) These three terms—*samhanach*,
uamh dhuine, and *ciuthach*—all seem to indicate one and the same
race of people. And these are probably the people referred to by
Pennant when he says, speaking of the civilised races of the

there is in Iceland a certain *Tröllakyrkia* (literally
"the dwarfs' church ") which is translated "the
giants' church." [1] For these reasons, then, I do
not regard any reference to the Fians as "giants"
as indicating that they were of tall stature;
although I see no objection to the assumption
that they were savages and cave-dwellers.

Fians, then, are closely connected with the
"little people" called "Fairies." The connection
between Fians and Picts is equally well marked.

Regarding them historically, Dr. Skene identi-

Hebrides in the beginning of the seventeenth century :—" Each
chieftain had his armour-bearer, who preceded his master in time
of war, and, by my author's (Timothy Pont's MS., Advocates'
Library, Edinburgh) account in time of peace; for they went armed
even to church, in the manner the North Americans do at present
[1772] in the frontier settlement, and for the same reason, the
dread of savages." (Pinkerton's *Voyages,* vol. iii. p. 322.)

[1] Hibbert's " Description of the Shetland Islands," Edinburgh,
1822, pp. 444-451. With regard to the " Dwarfie Stone" of Hoy,
the following references may be given :—" Jo. Ben," 1529, at p. 449
of Barry's "History of the Orkney Islands," 2nd ed., London,
1808 ; and other writers subsequent to 1529. These speak of this
stone as the abode of a "giant." Sir Walter Scott (*The Pirate,*
Note P.) and many others invariably say " a dwarf."

Note also J. F. Campbell (*W. H. Tales,* p. xcix) : " The Highland giants were not so big, but that their conquerors wore their
clothes." Also the dwarf in Ramsay's " Evergreen " who says that
he was engendered " of giants' kind."

fies the Fians with one or other of two historical
races believed to have occupied Ireland before the
coming of the Gaels.   These two races are known
in Irish story as the Tuatha De and the Cruithné.[1]
Now, the Tuatha De *are* the Fairies of Ireland.[2]
Therefore, according to Dr. Skene, the Fians were
either Fairies or Cruithné.   Now, Cruithné is
simply a Gaelic name for the Picts.   Consequently,
the Fians were either Fairies or Picts—according
to Dr. Skene.   In one traditional story, already
referred to, the Fians seem to be unhesitatingly
regarded as Picts.   This story, obtained in
Sutherlandshire, tells how a certain king lived for
a year with a *banshee*, or fairy woman,[3] by whom
he had a son.   When this son grew up he went
to the country of the Fians,[4] and there he entered

---

[1] *Dean of Lismore's Book*, p. lxxvi.; *Celt. Scot.*, vol. i. p. 131 ;
vol. iii. chap. iii. ; &c.

[2] *Celt. Scot.* iii. 106–7.

[3] In this tale, the phonetic spelling *ben-ee* shows the unusual
aspirated form *bean-shithe*. She is elsewhere spoken of as the
Lady of Innse Uaine, and her son is the hero of the tale *Gille nan
Cochla-Craicinn*.

[4] According to a clergyman of the seventeenth century, the
Hebrides and a part of the Western Highlands constituted "the
country of the Fians." (*Testimony of Tradition*, p. 45.)

into the service of their king, who was no other than the celebrated Oisin. The Gaelic narrator calls him "Oisin, Righ na Feinne," that is, "Ossian, King of the Fians"; but the collector of the story,[1] who had no doubt obtained the translation on the spot, renders *Righ na Feinne* as "King of the Picts." No explanation or comment is given, and one is therefore led to infer that in Sutherland-shire *Feinne* is without question regarded as a Gaelic name for the Picts. This identity is, indeed, borne out otherwise. There is a Gaelic saying in Glenlyon, Perthshire, to the effect that "Fin had twelve castles" in that glen, and the remains of these "castles," all said to have been built by him and his Fians, and of which one in particular is styled "Castle Fin,"[2] are known to the English-speaking people of Scotland as "Picts'" houses. For they belong to a peculiar class of structures, all radically alike, and all known, in certain districts, as "Picts' houses." The term "Picts' house" is unknown in the Hebrides, says

[1] Miss Dempster : "The Folk-Lore of Sutherlandshire," Folk-Lore Journal, vol. vi. 1888, p. 174.

[2] *Proc. of the Soc. of Antiq. of Scot.*, vol. vii. p. 294.

one writer. " In the Hebrides tradition is entirely
silent concerning the Picts : . . . there the Fenian
heroes are the builders of the duns."[1] Yet the
self-same class of building is elsewhere assigned
to the Picts. To these structures I shall presently
refer more particularly ; but it is enough to note
in passing that, just as Oisin, King of the Fians,
is translated into Ossian, King of the Picts, so the
dwellings ascribed to the Fians in one locality, are
in another said to have been made and inhabited
by the Picts.

Fians, then, are associated or identified with
Fairies, and also with Picts. To complete my
equilateral triangle, the Picts ought also to be
regarded as Fairies, or as akin to them.

This undoubtedly is a popular belief. The
earliest alleged reference of this kind is placed by
one writer in the middle of the fifteenth century,
before the Orkney Islands had passed from the
crown of Denmark to the crown of Scotland. A
manuscript of the then Bishop of Orkney, dated
Kirkwall 1443, states that when Harald Haarfagr
conquered the Orkneys in the ninth century, the

---

[1] *Proc. Soc. Antiq. Scot.*, vol. vii. pp. 165 and 192.

inhabitants were the two "nations" of the *Papæ*
and the *Peti*, both of whom were exterminated.
By the former name is understood the Irish
missionaries : the *Peti* were certainly the Picts,
or Pehts.[1] Now, of these Picts of Orkney it is
said, that they "were only a little exceeding pigmies in stature, and worked wonderfully in the
construction of their cities, evening and morning,
but in mid-day, being quite destitute of strength,
they hid themselves through fear in little houses
under ground."[2]

---

[1] "They are plainly no other than the Peihts, Picts, or Piks
. . . . . the Scandinavian writers generally call the Piks Peti, or
Pets : one of them uses the term Petia, instead of Pictland (Saxo-
Gram.) ; and, besides, the frith that divides Orkney from Caithness
is usually denominated Petland Fiord in the Icelandic Sagas or
histories." (Barry's *Orkney*, p. 115.)

[2] *Proc. of the Soc. of Antiq. of Scot.*, vol. iii. p. 141 : also
vol. vii. p. 191. This quotation is made by the late Captain
Thomas, R.N., a sound archæologist ; but I have to add that in
the document of 1443, as given in Barry's *Orkney* (2nd ed.,
London, 1808, pp. 401-419), while I find the statement as to the
two native races, I find nothing about the stature or habits of the
Picts. Captain Thomas twice quotes his statement, and as at one
place he refers, not to the Bishop of 1443, but (vol. iii. p. 141)
to "the Earl of Orkney's chaplain, writing about 1460," it is
possible he had two manuscripts of the fifteenth century in
view.

[SUPPLEMENTARY NOTE.—The Bishop's words are as follows :—

The exact date of this statement is at present
doubtful, but it is quite in accordance with the
widespread ideas held throughout Scotland and
Northumberland with regard to the Picts : that
they were great as builders, but were of very low
stature, and closely akin to Fairies.[1] Moreover,
they are famous for doing their work during the
night. Whatever be the explanation of the above
curious statement that at mid-day they lost their
strength and withdrew to their underground
houses, it is at any rate interesting to compare
with it the remark made by the traveller Pennant
as he was passing along Glenorchy in 1772. This
is the entry in his journal :—" See frequently on
the road-sides small verdant hillocks, styled by
the common people shi an (*sithean*), or the Fairy-
haunt, because here, say they, the fairies, who
love not the glare of day, make their retreat after

" *Istas insulas primitus Peti et Pape inhabitabant.   Horum alteri
scilicet Peti parvo superantes pigmeos statura in structuris urbium
vespere et mane mira operantes, meredie vero cunctis viribus prorsus
destituti in subterraneis domunculis pre timore latuerunt.*"—From
his treatise *De Orcadibus Insulis*, reprinted in the " Bannatyne
Miscellany, 1855, p. 33.]

[1] *Testimony of Tradition*, pp. 58-60, 65, 67-74, 79-80.

the celebration of their nocturnal revels." [1]   Now,
as the "Picts' houses" are, to outward appearance,
"small verdant hillocks," the parallel is very exact.
With these two references compare also the mention, in a quaint old gazetteer printed at Cambridge
in 1693,[2] of the tribe of the " Germara," defined as
"a people of the Celtæ, who in the day-time
cannot see." Although the author usually gives
the sources of his information, in this instance he
gives none. But the statement agrees perfectly
with the belief found everywhere throughout
Northern Europe that " the dwarfs could not
bear daylight, and during the day hid in their
holes." [3] It really seems impossible to avoid the
inference that all this was perfectly true. When
Leif went down into the underground house in
Ireland, he could not see at first, though at length
he saw in the obscurity the glimmer of his oppo-
nent's sword. Consequently, the denizens and

---

[1] Pennant's Second Tour in Scotland ; Pinkerton's *Voyages*,
London, 1809, p. 368.

[2] Linguæ Romanæ, Dictionarium, Luculentum Novum.

[3] Du Chaillu : *Land of the Midnight Sun*, vol. ii. pp. 421-2. This
also is one of the articles of belief in Shetland, with regard to the
trows, as the trolls are there called.

builders of these subterranean retreats must
either have had something very like "cat's eyes,"
or else they must in general have had numerous
lamps burning. This will be understood by an
examination of one or two of the accompanying
diagrams. It seems to me beyond question that
a people living this underground life must have
differed very distinctly from ourselves in the
matter of vision ; and to them the brightness of
noonday must have been blinding. This physical
fact—if it be a fact—would explain much that is
otherwise strange and incredible in the traditions
relating to the Picts—or Pechts, as they were
formerly called in Scotland. However, it is
sufficient for my present purpose to note that
this peculiarity associates, and indeed identifies,
the Picts with the dwarfs or fairies of tradition.

Having thus shown that Fians, Fairies, and
Picts are so closely associated as to be, in some
aspects, almost indistinguishable from one another,
I shall now refer to the structures which are popularly believed to have been their dwellings. Some
of these are wholly underground, others partly so,
and others quite above ground. In many other

ways, also, they vary. But all of them are unquestionably links in one special style of structure; of which the most marked feature, or at
any rate that which is common to all, is the use
of what is called the "cyclopean" arch. This is
formed by the overlapping of the stones in the
wall until they almost meet at the dome or apex
of the building, when a heavy "keystone" completes this rude arch. The principle of the arch
proper was obviously quite unknown to the
originators of such structures.

Of the various Hebridean specimens of these
buildings, very interesting and complete descriptions have been given by the late Captain Thomas,
R.N.,[1] and Sir Arthur Mitchell,[2] who visited some
of them together in 1866. Referring to the most
modern examples of this kind of structure, the
latter writer says :—"They are commonly spoken
of as beehive houses, but their Gaelic name is
bo'h or *bothan*. They are now only used as temporary residences or shealings by those who herd

---

[1] *Proc. of Soc. of Antiq. of Scot.* (First Series), vol. iii. pp. 127–
144 ; vol. vii. pp. 153–195.

[2] *The Past in the Present*, Edinburgh, 1880, pp. 58 72.

the cattle at their summer pasturage ; but at a
time not very remote they are believed to have
been the permanent dwellings of the people."
And he thus describes his first sight of the bee-
hive houses :—

" I do not think I ever came upon a scene which more
surprised me, and I scarcely know where or how to begin my
description of it.

" By the side of a burn which flowed through a little grassy
glen . . . . we saw two small round hive-like hillocks, not
much higher than a man, joined together, and covered with
grass and weeds.   Out of the top of one of them a column of
smoke slowly rose, and at its base there was a hole about three
feet high and two feet wide, which seemed to lead into the
interior of the hillock—its hollowness, and the possibility of
its having a human creature within it being thus suggested.
There was no one, however, actually within the *bo'h*, the three
girls, when we came in sight, being seated on a knoll by the
burn-side, but it was really in the inside of these two green
hillocks that they slept, and cooked their food, and carried on
their work, and—dwelt, in short."[1]

These two " green hillocks," and other structures of the same nature, are shown in the
accompanying diagrams[2] (Plates I.-XVI.), which
explain their formation better than any written

---

[1] *The Past in the Present*, p. 59.

[2] Reproduced by permission of the Society of Antiquaries of
Scotland.

description. It is enough here to state that they are built of rough stone, without any mortar. "Though the stone walls are very thick," says my authority (p. 62), "they are covered on the outside with turf, which soon becomes grassy like the land round about, and thus secures perfect wind and water tightness." Sometimes they occur in groups, as those shown in Plate III.; of which scene Captain Thomas justly remarks that "at first sight it may be taken for a picture of a Hottentot village rather than a hamlet in the British Isles." [1] Here there is little or no grassy covering outside, however; and consequently none of the hillock-like effect. But this is very well shown in Plates VI. and VIII. Of the "agglomeration of beehives" pictured in the latter, Sir Arthur Mitchell observes:—" It has several entrances, and would accommodate many families, who might be spoken of as living in one mound, rather than under one roof " (*op. cit.* pp. 64-5). Of another such dwelling, now ruined, he says that it could have accommodated " from forty to fifty people."

---

[1] *Proc. Soc. Antiq. Scot.*, vol. iii. p. 137.

This last, however (Plates XI. and XII.),
represents another variety of earth-house, the
chambered mound or beehive, with an underground gallery leading to it. Of this kind two
examples are here shown. And in Plates I.
and XIII. will be seen specimens of wholly subterranean structures. It is difficult, and indeed
hardly necessary, to distinguish between one
variety and another of what is practically the
same kind of building; but to this last class the
term "earth-house" is most frequently accorded
in Scotland. In the broader dialect it is "yird-
house" or "eirde-house," which at once recalls
the form "jord-hus" in the saga which tells of
Leif's adventure underground in Ireland. The
term *weem* is also applied to these places in
Scotland. This is merely a quickened pro-
nunciation of the Gaelic *uam* (or *uamh*), a cave;
and it reminds one that, both in Gaelic and in
English, the word "cave" is by no means
restricted to a *natural* cavity. Indeed, one of
the two artificial structures under consideration
is known as *Uamh Sgalabhad,* "the *cave* of
Sgalabhad." Another old Gaelic name for those

underground galleries is "*tung* or *tunga*";[1] while another name, by which they are known in Lewis is *tigh fo thalaimh*,[2] or "house beneath the ground."

"Martin, in his description of the Western Islands, printed in 1703, when their use would appear to have been still remembered, speaks of them [these underground structures] as 'little stone-houses, built under ground, called earth-houses, which served to hide a few people and their goods in time of war.'"[3] Dean Monro writes, "There is sundry coves and holes in the earth, coverit with hedder above, quhilk fosters many rebellis in the country of the North head of Ywst" [North Uist].[4] "From O'Flaherty's description of West Connaught, written in 1684, it appears," observes Captain Thomas,[5] but

---

[1] *Proc. Soc. Antiq. Scot.*, vol. vii. p. 168 *n*. This appears to me to be a phonetic spelling of the *diongna* mentioned in the passage relating to the plunderings of the Danes in the ninth century.

[2] *Ibid.* p. 171. On the same page, the form *tigh talamhant* is given.

[3] *Chambers's Encyclopædia*, new ed., s.v. Earth-house.

[4] Quoted in *Proc. Soc. Antiq. Scot.*, vii. 172. The reference is "Ag. Rep. Heb. p. 782."

[5] *Op. cit.* vol. iii. p. 140.

referring more strictly to the beehive-house, "that this style of dwelling had already become archaic." For, although that writer mentions certain "cloghans" as being still inhabited, holding forty men in some cases, yet he says they were "so ancient that nobody knows how long ago any of them were made." Of the underground galleries another writer says : " It has been doubted if these houses were ever really used as places of abode. . . . . But as to this there can be no real doubt. The substances found in many of them have been the accumulated *débris* of food used by man. . . . . Ornaments of bronze have been found in a few of them, and beads of streaked glass. In some cases the articles found would indicate that the occupation of these houses had come down to comparatively recent times." [1]

In conclusion, these remarks of Captain Thomas, who made so thorough a study of the subject, may be quoted :—

" The Pict's house on the Holm of Papay [Orkney] would have held, besides the chiefs at each end, all the families in [the island of] Papay Westray when it was built. Maes howe [2]

[1] John Stuart, LL.D., *Proc. Soc. Antiq. Scot.*, viii. pp. 23 *et seq.*
[2] Plates XIV.-XVI. Compare also Plates XVII.-XIX.

was for three families—grandees, no doubt; but the numbers
it was intended to hold in the *beds* may be learned by comparing them with the Amazon's House, St. Kilda."[1]

" I consider the relation between the *boths* [beehive houses]
and the Picts' houses of the Orkneys (and elsewhere) to be
evident—the same method of forming the arch, the low and
narrow doors and passages, the enormous thickness of the
walls, when compared with the interior accommodation—exist
in both. When a *both* is covered with green turf it becomes a
chambered tumulus, and when buried by drifting sand it is a
subterranean Pict's house. . . . . I regard the comparatively
large Picts' houses of the Orkneys as the pastoral residence of
the Pictish lord, fitted to contain his numerous family and
dependents. Such an one exists on the Holm of Papa
Westray, which, according to the Highland method of stow-
age, would certainly contain a whole clan. When writing the
description of it, I had not made acquaintance with a people
who would close the door to keep in the smoke, or that
nested in holes in a wall like sand-martins. . . .

" But the *both* of the Long Island is only the lodging of the
common man or ' Tuathanach,' and is consequently of small
dimensions, and not remarkable for comfort. If the modern
Highland proprietor or large farmer should ever be induced to
lead a pastoral life, and adopt a Pictish architecture in his
residence, we might again see a tumulus of twenty feet in
height, with its long low passage leading into a large hall with
beehive cells on both sides."[2]

But the point of all this is that these dwellings,
whether above ground or below, are known as

---

[1] *Op. cit.*, vII. 191.   [2] *Op. cit.*, III. 133.

Picts' Houses, Fairy Halls, Elf Hillocks, "the hidden places of *Fians and Fairies.*" Thus, the three titles which I have shown to be associated in other ways are all given to the alleged builders and occupiers of those very archaic and peculiar structures.

It is true that, in their most modern form, some of those dwellings are still inhabited for months at a time. And their inhabitants are neither Fians, Fairies nor Picts. But it is among those people that stories of Fians and Fairies are most rife, and many claim an actual descent from them. And although they are certainly not pigmies, yet they live in a district in which the *small* type of this heterogeneous nation of ours is still quite discernible ; and that part of the island of Lewis (Uig), which has longest retained those places as dwellings, is inhabited by a caste whom other Hebrideans describe as small, and regard as different from themselves.[1] Dr. Beddoe states that the tallest people in the United Kingdom

---

[1] *Proceedings of the Society of Antiquaries of Scotland,* vol. iii. (First Series), p. 129. The district of Barvas is specially referred to by Captain Thomas.

are to be found in a certain village in Galloway,
where a six-foot man is perfectly common, and
many are above that height. It is quite certain
that such men could not "nest like sand-martins"
in the holes in the wall described by Captain
Thomas. And, in proportion as such Galloway
men are to the modern Hebridean mound-dwellers, so are these to the much more archaic race
with whom the oldest structures are associated.
For a study of the dimensions of these will show
that they could not have been conceived, and
would not have been built or inhabited by any
but a race of actual dwarfs ; as tradition says they
were.

APPENDIX.

MOST of the illustrations here given are reproductions of some of the plates accompanying Captain Thomas's papers in the *Proceedings of the Society of Antiquaries of Scotland.* In explanation of their details the following extracts may be made.

PLATE I. (Frontispiece).—*Uamh Sgalabhad, South Uist.*
(From Plate XXXV. of Vol. VII. of *Proceedings of the Society of Antiquaries of Scotland,* First Series.)

Captain Thomas thus describes his descent into and exploration of this earth-house :—" An irregular hole was pointed out by the little lassie before alluded to, and some of my party quickly disappeared below ground. As they did not immediately return, I thought it was time to follow, and squeezing through the ruinated entrance (*a*), I entered the usual kind of gallery, which descended into the ground at a sharp angle. At the bottom, on the right-hand side, was the usual guard-cell (*b*); the sides of dry-stone masonry, but the end was the face of a rock *in situ.* Proceeding on, the roof rose and the gallery widened to what was the main chamber (*c*), which was 7 feet high under the apex of the dome, and 4 feet broad. Upon the west side of this chamber, and about 2 feet from the ground, is a recess, about 2 feet square and 4 feet long. At the further end, and in the same right line,

the gallery (*d*) became low (2½ feet) and narrow (2 feet).
Again the roof rose, and the gallery widened till stopt, in face,
by a large transported rock (*f*); to the right of the rock a
rectangular chamber (*e*), 2 feet broad, extended 4 feet, and
ended against rock *in situ*. Round, and beyond the rock (*f*),
the wall of the left side of the gallery was built, but the passage
was so narrow (*g*) that I contented myself by looking through
it. This incomprehensible narrowness is a feature in the
buildings of this period. Some of Captain Otter's officers
pushed through into the small chamber (*h*); beyond this the
gallery was ruinated and impassable ; the total length explored
was 45 feet." [1]

PLATE II.—*Bee-Hive Houses at Uig, Lewis.*
(From Plate XXXI. of Vol. VII. of *Proceedings of the Society of
Antiquaries of Scotland,* First Series.)

Fig. 8. Captain Thomas selects this as " the most modern,
and at the same time the last, in all probability, that will be
constructed in this manner "—viz., " roofed by the horizontal
or cyclopean arch, *i.e.,* by a system of overlapping stones."
" The woman who was living in it [about 1869] told us it was
built for his shieling by Dr. Macaulay's grandfather, who was
tacksman [leaseholder] of Linshader . . . . and I conclude
that it was made about ninety years back." [2]

Fig. 9. Sir Arthur Mitchell says of this compound " bee-
hive" house :—"The greatest height of the living room—in
its centre, that is—was scarcely 6 feet. In no part of the
dairy was it possible to stand erect. The door of communication between the two rooms was so small that we could get

---

[1] *Proc. Soc. Antiq. Scot.,* vol. vii. (First Series), pp. 167–8.
[2] *Op. cit.,* p. 161.

PLATE II.

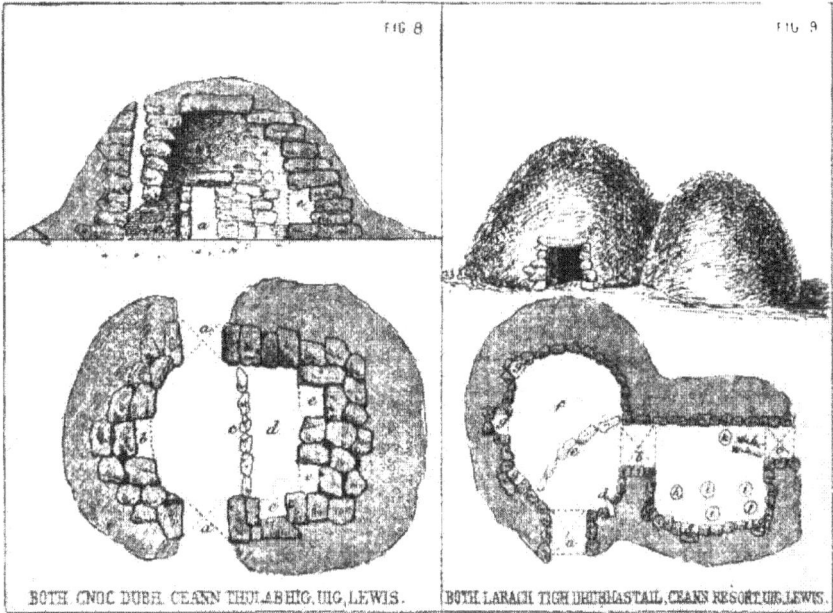

FIG 8.

FIG 9.

BOTH GNOC DUBH. CEANN THULABHIG. UIG, LEWIS.

BOTH LARACH TIGH DHUBHASTAIL, CEANN RESORT UIG, LEWIS.

FIG. 8.

FIG. 9.

"It is of a bee-hive form, about 18 feet in diameter, 9 feet high, and covered with green turf outside."

a a. doors; 3 feet high, "higher and better formed than is usual."
b. fireplace (having a chimney above, which is exceptional).
c. row of stones marking off *d.*
d. bed on floor.
e e e, small recesses in wall.

Dwelling and Dairy joined, "of the usual bee-hive shape, and green with the growing turf." Dairy "6 feet square on floor, but roundish externally."

a. doorway; "easily closed with a creel, a bundle of heather, or a straw mat."
b. "a very low interior doorway."
c. doorway of dairy.
d. fireplace: "the smoke escaping through a hole in the apex of the dome."
e. "the usual row of stones."
. "a litter of hay and rushes for a bed."
g. niches in wall.
i j k l. various utensils.

PLATE III.

BEE-HIVE HOUSES, FIDIGIDH IOCHDRACH, UIG, LEWIS, HEBRIDES. Inhabited 1859.

PLATE IV.

Fig. 1, 2

Height, 9 feet.

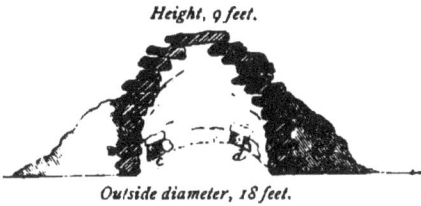

Outside diameter, 18 feet.

Fig. 3, 4, 5, 6

Elevation of Cell or Bed-Place.

b. Cell or Bed-Place. Length, 4½ feet; breadth, 1½ to 2 feet; height, 2 feet 4 inches

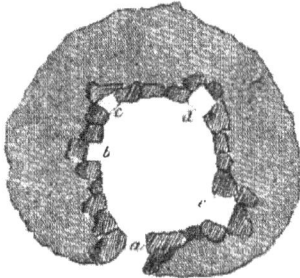

Plan and Elevation of A

Scale of Feet

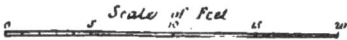

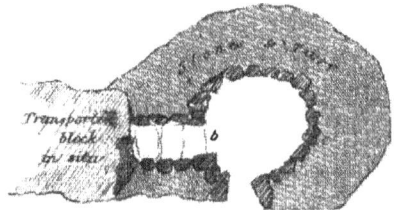

Plan and Elevation of B

BEEHIVE-HOUSES (BOTHAN) MEABHAG, FOREST OF HARRIS.

PLATE V.

a. "*scarcely*
18 in. wide."

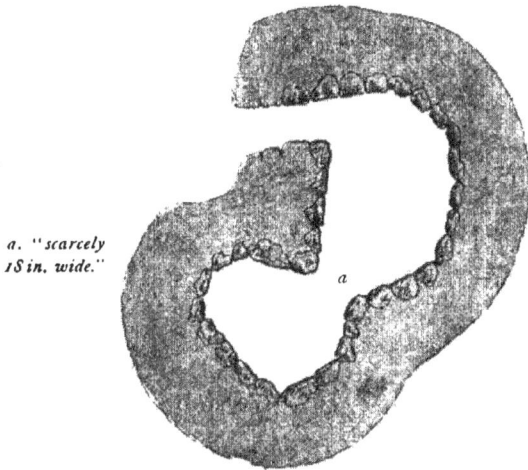

GROUND PLAN OF RUINED *BOTH* AT BAILE
FHLODAIDH, ON THE NORTH SIDE OF
THE ISLAND OF BENBECULA.

PLATE VI.

"A hole (*e*), called the Farlos, is left in the apex of the roof for the escape of the smoke, and is closed with a turf or flat stone as requisite."

Height of Dome, 7 feet.

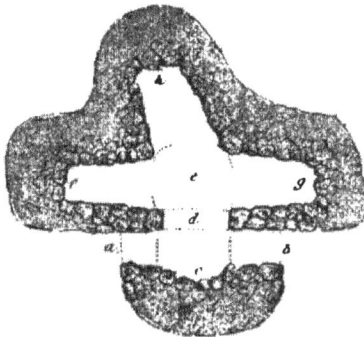

a, b. Doorways.
c. Fireplace.
d. Row of stones for seats.
e. Centre. (Distance from e to end of cells, 7 feet.)
f, g, h. Cells or bed-places.
f is "2 feet wide and 15 inches high at the inner end; is 5 feet long and 3 feet high at the mouth. The opposite cell (g) is of the same dimensions. The third cell (h) is 4 feet wide at the mouth, 5 feet long, decreasing to 2½ feet wide at the head, where it is 16 inches high."

SECTIONAL VIEW AND GROUND PLAN OF MOUND DWELLING,
CALLED *BOTH STACSEAL*, SITUATED MIDWAY
BETWEEN STORNOWAY AND CARLO-
WAY, LEWIS, HEBRIDES.

The above is given by Captain Thomas as an example of such dwellings "having oven-like bed-places around the internal area. . . . . This interesting summer house illustrates the most antique form of dormitory; but in the winter houses the floor of the bedroom was raised three or four feet above the ground." (Compare the side cells in Maes-How, Orkney.)

through it only by creeping. The great thickness of the walls, 6 to 8 feet, gave this door, or passage of communication, the look of a tunnel, and made the creeping through it very real. The creeping was only a little less real in getting through the equally tunnel-like, though somewhat wider and loftier passage, which led from the open air into the first or dwelling room." [1]

PLATE III.—*Bee-Hive Houses at Uig, inhabited in* 1859.
(From Plate XII. of Vol. III. of *Proceedings of the Society of Antiquaries of Scotland*, First Series.)
See p. 47, *ante.*

PLATE IV.—*Bee-Hive Houses at Meabhag, Forest of Harris.*
(From Plate X. of Vol. III. of *Proceedings of the Society of Antiquaries of Scotland*, First Series.)

At the date of Captain Thomas's visit (1861) a man was still living who had been born in one or other of these dwellings.

PLATE V.—*Ground Plan of Bee-Hive House, Island of Benbecula.*
(From Plate XXXII. of Vol. VII. of *Proceedings of the Society of Antiquaries of Scotland*, First Series.)

PLATE VI.—*Chambered Mound (Both Stacseal), near Stornoway, Lewis.*
(From Plate XXXII. of Vol. VII. of *Proceedings of the Society of Antiquaries of Scotland*, First Series.)

With reference to the *farlos*, or smoke-hole (otherwise " sky-light "), which, in this instance, is at a height of 7 feet from

[1] *The Past in the Present*, p. 60.

the floor of the dwelling, Captain Thomas remarks :—"A man, on standing upright, can often put his head out of the hole and look around " (*op. cit.*, vol. iii., p. 130 *n.*). This suggests the following story, told by Mr. J. F. Campbell (*West Highland Tales*, vol. ii., pp. 39–40):

"There was a woman in Baile Thangusdail, and she was out seeking a couple of calves ; and the night and lateness caught her, and there came rain and tempest, and she was seeking shelter. She went to a knoll with the couple of calves, and she was striking the tether-peg into it. The knoll opened. She heard a gleegashing *(gliogadaich)* as if a pot-hook were clashing beside a pot. She took wonder, and she stopped striking the tether-peg. A woman put out her head and all above her middle, and she said, 'What business hast thou to be troubling this tulman [mound] in which I make my dwelling?' 'I am taking care of this couple of calves, and I am but weak. Where shall I go with them?' 'Thou shalt go with them to that breast down yonder. Thou wilt see a tuft of grass. If thy couple of calves eat that tuft of grass, thou wilt not be a day without a milk cow as long as thou art alive, because thou hast taken my counsel.'

"As she said, she never was without a milk cow after that, and she was alive fourscore and fifteen years after the night that was there."

PLATES VII. AND VIII.—" *Agglomeration of Bee-Hives* " *at Uig, Lewis.*

(From Plates XV. and XVI. of Vol. III. of *Proceedings of the Society of Antiquaries of Scotland*, First Series.)

"By far the most singular of all these structures, and probably unique in the Long Island, is at Gearraidh na h-Airde

PLATE VII.

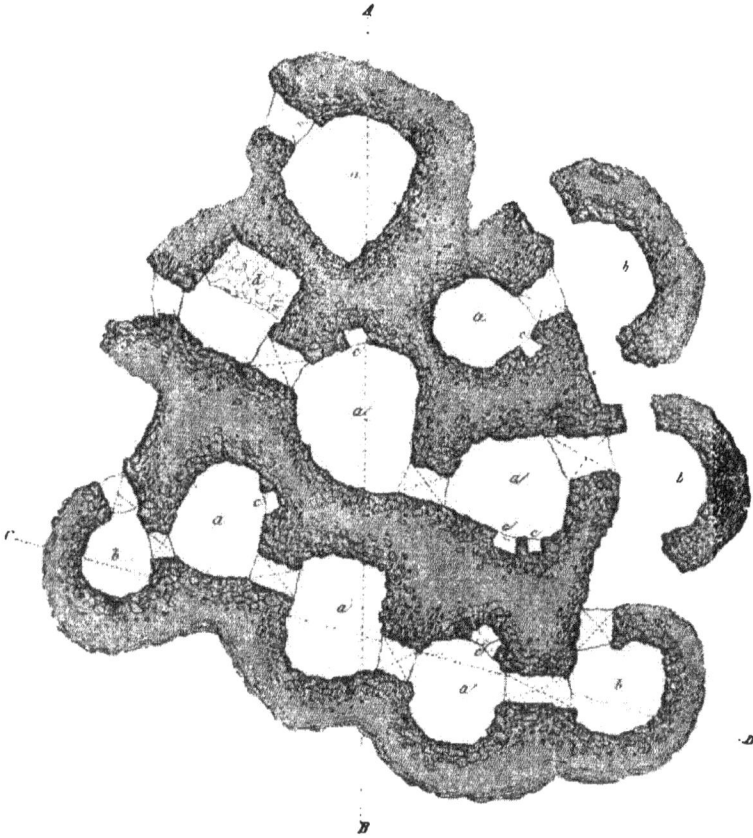

a. Dwelling apartments
b. Frogorion or Porch
c. Cailean or Milk cupboards
d. Stanebonch or Bedplace

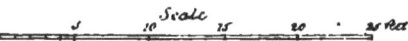

Scale
5   10   15   20   25 feet

A.B. Line of Section
C.D. View as represented
or restored

GROUND PLAN OF *BOTHAN GEARRAIDH NA H'AIRDE MOIRE* UIG
LEWIS, HEBRIDES.

PLATE VIII.

Section A B

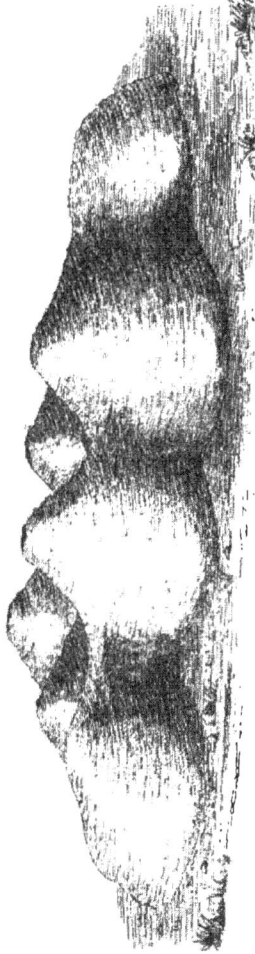

View of Line C D if restored.

SECTION AND ELEVATION OF *BOTHAN GEARRAIDH NA H'AIRDE MOIRE*, UIG, LEWIS, HEBRIDES, AND VIEW OF SAME IF RESTORED.

PLATE IX.

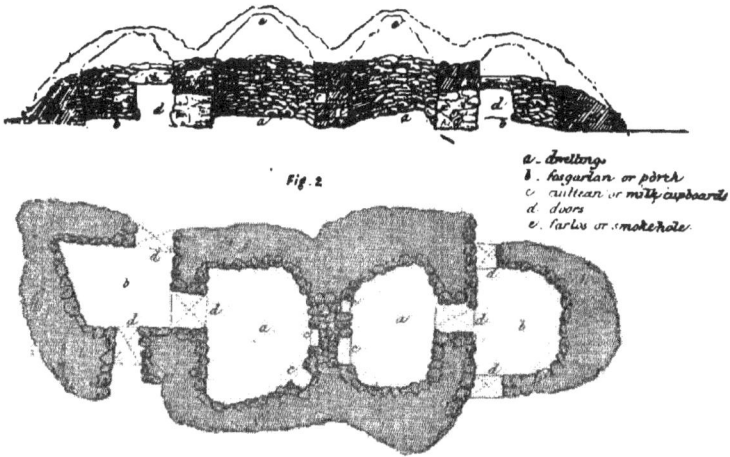

Fig. 2

a. dwellings
b. fosgarian or porch
c. cuiltean or milk cupboards
d. doors
e. farlis or smokehole

PLAN AND ELEVATION OF A BOTH
at Gearraidh Aird Mhor, Uig, Lewis

"One of a group of three at the garry of Aird Mhor, close to the shore and near the mouth of Loch Resort, Uig, Lewis. This compound *both* has evidently been intended for two related families . . . . but there is no interior communication between the dwellings." (*Op. cit., p. 144.*)

PLATE X.

FIG. 15.

d 5 feet.

e

c 5 feet.

13 feet.

b Length about 20 feet.

14 feet.

a

7 feet.

Scale of Feet

Length about 20 feet.
About 2½ feet square.

b

6½ ft. high.

2 × 2

5 ft. high

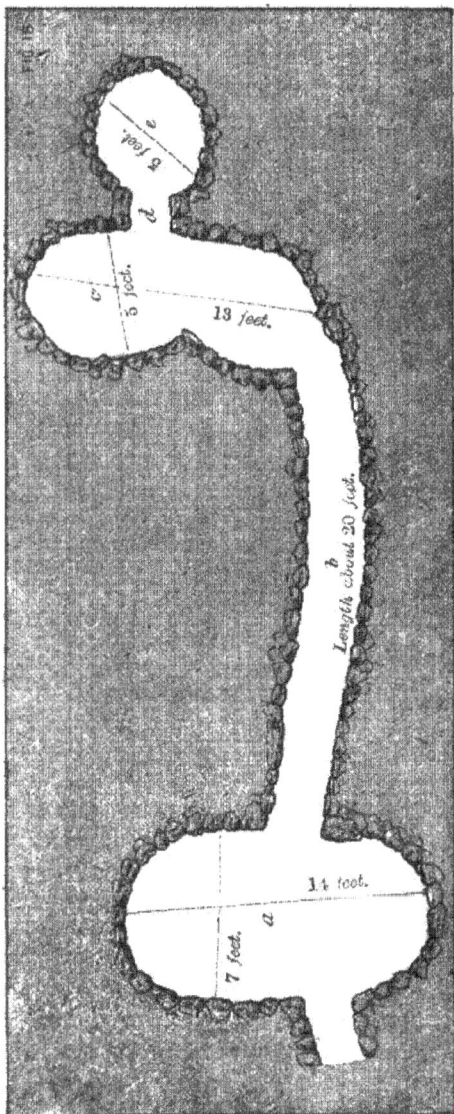

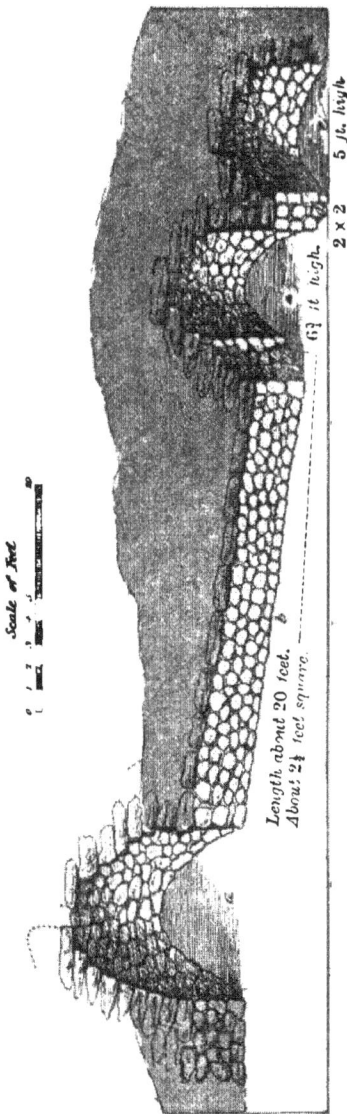

GROUND PLAN AND SECTIONAL VIEW OF SEMI-SUBTERRANEAN *BOTH* AND UNDERGROUND GALLERY, MEAL NA H-UAMH, MOL A DEAS, HUISHNISH, ISLAND OF SOUTH UIST.

Moire, on the shore of Loch Resort. I cannot describe it
better than by bidding you suppose twelve individual bee-hive
huts all built touching each other, with doors and passages
from one to the other. The diameter of this gigantic booth is
46 feet, and [it] is nearly circular in plan. The height of the
doors and passages about 2½ feet; and under the smokehole
(*farlos*), in two of the chambers, the height was 6½ feet. . . . .
I am informed that, so late as 1823, this *both* was inhabited by
four families." (Captain Thomas, *Proc. Soc. Antiq. Scot.*,
vol. iii., p. 139.)

PLATE IX.—*Compound "Both" situated near the above.*
(From Plate XIV. of Vol. III. of *Proceedings of the Society of
Antiquaries of Scotland*, First Series.)

PLATE X.—*"Both" and Underground Gallery at Meall na
h-Uamh, Huishnish, South Uist.*
(From Plate XXXIII. of Vol. VII. of *Proceedings of the Society of
Antiquaries of Scotland*, First Series.)

"I have next to notice," says Captain Thomas (*op. cit.*,
p. 164), "that form of bo'h, Pict's house, or clochan, whichever name may be adopted by archæologists, to which a
hypogeum or subterranean gallery is attached. . . . . [The
present example] is in South Uist, about half a mile inland
from Moll a Deas (South Beach); and the Moll is about one
mile and a half to the south of Husinish (Husness, *i.e.*, House-
ness). The site of the bo'h is called Meall na [h-] Uamh, or
Cave Lump [more correctly, the Mound of the Cave, or
'Weem.'] It consists of a partly excavated oval dwelling
chamber (*a*), 7 feet by 14 feet on the floor; the dome roof has
fallen in; there are two *cuiltean*, or niches in the wall. A low
curved subterranean passage (*b*), about 2½ feet square and

20 feet in length, leads into an elongated bee-hive chamber (*c*), 13 feet by 5 feet, and 6¾ feet high ; from thence an entrance (*d*), 2 feet by 2 feet, admits to a small circular chamber or cell (*e*), 5 feet in diameter and 5 feet high. The main passage inclines downwards, so that the floor of the second chamber (*c*) is nearly 3 feet lower than that of the first (*a*) ; and that of the inner one (*e*) a foot below the second (*c*)."

PLATES XI. AND XII.—*"Both" and Underground Gallery at Huishnish, South Uist.*
(From Plates XXXIV. and XXXV. of Vol. VII. of *Proceedings of the Society of Antiquaries of Scotland*, First Series.)

" An ancient dwelling, semi-subterranean, exists at Nisibost, Harris [and is described in vol. iii. of the *Proceedings*, p. 140]. . . . . A still finer example exists near to Meall na h-Uamh, in South Uist. . . . . The bo'h, or Pict's house, as it would be called in the Orkneys—but the name is unknown in the Long Island—that I am about to describe lies less than half a mile above the shepherd's house ; but so little curiosity had that individual that he was entirely unacquainted with it ; and I believe it would never have been found by us but for a little terrier (in its etymological sense, of course) of a daughter. The child was only acquainted with the two here drawn [of which the other—viz., *Uamh Sgalabhad*, is here reproduced as Plate I., frontispiece] ; but there may be many more waiting the researches of the zealous antiquary." (Captain Thomas, *op. cit.*, p. 165.)

PLATE XIII.—*Underground Gallery at Paible, Taransay, Harris.*
(From Plate XXIX. of Vol. VII. of *Proceedings of the Society of Antiquaries of Scotland*, First Series.)

Describing this earth-house, Captain Thomas says :—" The

PLATE XI.

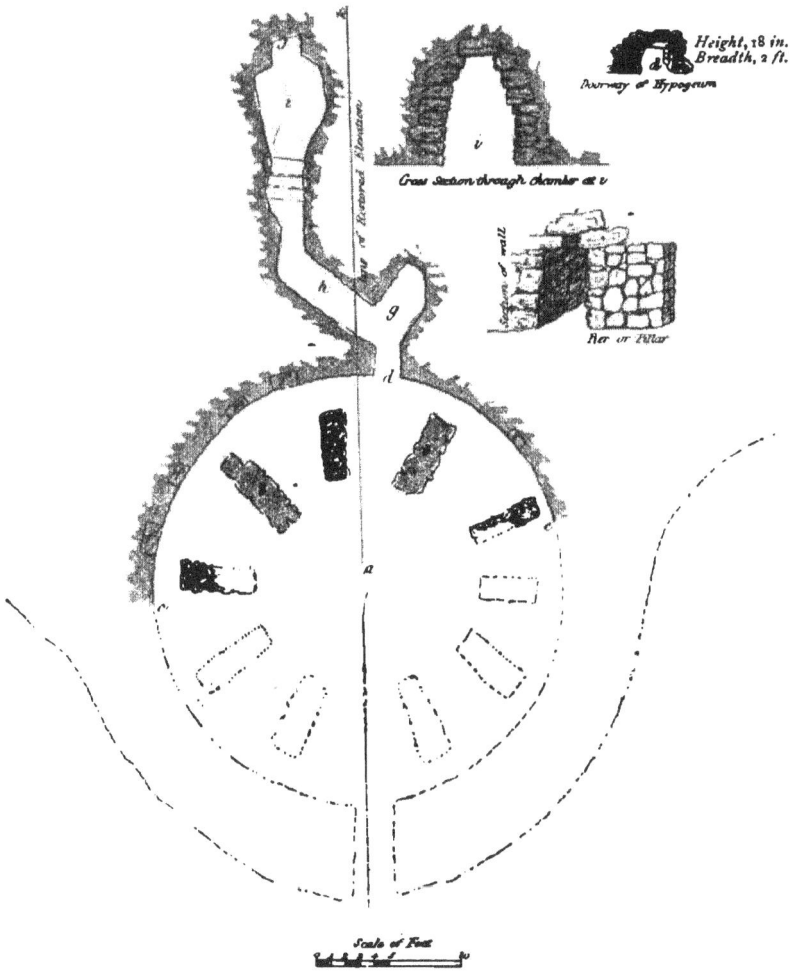

Height, 18 in.
Breadth, 2 ft.

Doorway of Hypogeum

Cross Section through Chamber at v

Pier or Pillar

Scale of Feet

GROUND PLAN OF *BOTH* AND UNDERGROUND GALLERY, OR. *TIGH LAIR*,
NEAR MOL A DEAS, HUISHNISH, ISLAND OF SOUTH UIST.

PLATE XII.

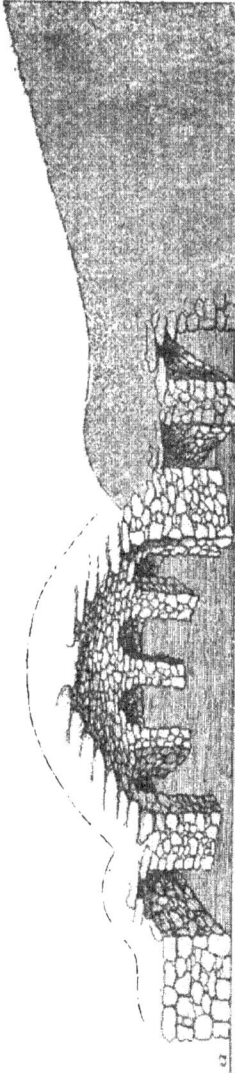

"These piers were about 4 feet high, 4 feet to 6 feet long, and 1½ foot to 2 feet broad; and there was a passage of from 1 foot to 2 feet in width between the wall and them."

RESTORED ELEVATION OF ANCIENT BOTH AND SECTION OF HYPOGEUM OR TIGH LAIR, ON THE LINE a, k NEAR MOL A DEAS, HUISHNISH, SOUTH UIST.

"On a small, flattish terrace, where the hill sloped steeply, an area had been cleared by digging away the bank, so that the wall of the house, for nearly half its circumference, was the side of the hill, faced with stone. . . . The hypogeum or subterranean gallery is on a level with the floor, pierced towards the hill, and is entered by a very small doorway [marked d on Ground Plan, Plate XI.]. . . . . It is but 18 inches high and 2 feet broad, so that a very stout or large man could not get in." (Op. cit., pp. 166, 167.)

PLATE XIII.

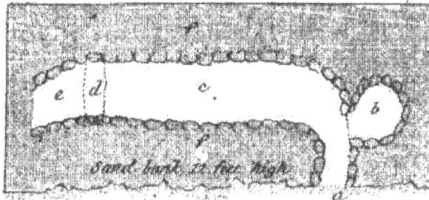

Guard-cell (2 feet
5 inches high, by
3 feet wide).

Sandy sea shore   Entrance.

GROUND PLAN AND ENTRANCE OF UNDERGROUND GALLERY
AT PAIBLE, TARANSAY, HARRIS.

"The drawing is from a photograph of the entrance, which is 2 feet 10 inches
high and 1½ foot broad. The sea flows up to it at high tides."

PLATE XIV.

MAES-HOW, ORKNEY.

PLATE XV.

Cell or Bed in Wall.

INTERIOR OF MAES-HOW, ORKNEY

(Facing inner doorway of gallery).

PLATE XVI.

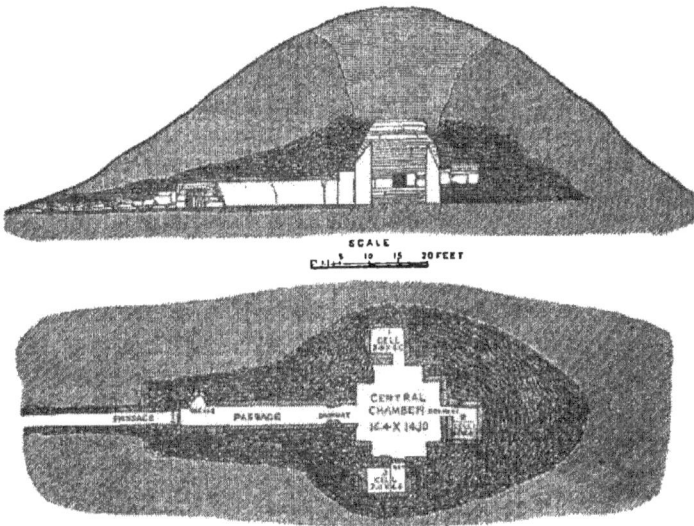

SECTIONAL VIEW AND GROUND PLAN OF MAES-HOW.

drawing is from a photograph of the entrance, which is 2 feet
10 inches high and 1½ foot broad. The sea flows up to it at
high tides. On crawling in, there is seen the usual guard-cell
(*b*), close beside the entrance, but so small that we may be
sure the sentinel, if there was one, must have been a light
weight; in fact, we are almost driven to the conclusion that
there were no Bantings in those days. This guard-cell is but
2 feet 5 inches high, and 3 feet in width. The gallery then
turns at a right angle to the left hand. We excavated it for
22 feet. . . . . When digging, we came upon two broken
stone dishes (corn-crushers?) now in the Museum [Society of
Antiquaries of Scotland]; and above the gallery were most of
the bones of a small ox, placed orderly together. . . . . Bones
of the seal were common, and a few of the eagle." (*Op. cit.*,
p. 169.)

PLATES XIV., XV., AND XVI.—*Maes-How, Orkney.*

These plates represent the "Pict's house" referred to by
Captain Thomas (pp. 50-51, *ante*), with regard to which he
says :—" Maes howe was for three families—grandees, no
doubt; but the numbers it was intended to hold in the *beds*
may be learned by comparing them with the Amazon's House,
St. Kilda."

The structure last named is described by Captain Thomas
and Mr. T. S. Muir in vol. iii. of the *Proceedings* (pp. 225-
228), where it is stated :—" The Amazon's House is of the
same class with our earliest stone buildings—belonging to the
era of cromlechs, stone-circles, Picts' castles, &c.; but while in
other parts of Britain the style and type have vanished for a
thousand years, in the Outer Hebrides we find them (in the
Bothan [*i.e.*, ' boths ' or ' bee-hive houses '] of Uig) continued

to the present day." The following additional remarks by
Captain Thomas are also of interest in this connection :—" It
appears that besides the Tigh na Bhanna ghaisgach (Ty-na-
Van-a-ghas-gec), or Amazon's House—and of whom all tradition, except her name, has gone—there are the remains of
other submerged dwellings and hypogea. Miss Euphemia
MacCrimmon, the oldest inhabitant of that far-off island, tells
that a certain Donald Macdonald and John Macqueen, on
passing a hillock, heard churning going on within. And about
thirty years ago, when digging into the hillock to make the
foundations of a new house, they discovered what seemed to
be the fairies' residence, built of stones inside, and holes in
the wall, or croops, as they call them, as in Airidh na
Bhannaghaisgach." [1]

It will be noticed that the " beds " in Maes-How are on a
higher level than the floor of the main chamber. " In the
winter houses," observes Captain Thomas,[2] " the floor of the
bed-place was raised 3 or 4 feet above the ground."

The original use of Maes-How is a matter of opinion, and
some have assumed it to belong to the class of sepulchral
mounds, although there is no evidence in support of this
belief. For many reasons, the opinions of Captain Thomas
are endorsed by the present writer. It may be added that,
prior to 1861, when the mound was opened, local tradition
had declared that it was the residence of a " hog-boy," or
mound-dweller.

---

[1] *Proc. Soc. Antiq. Scot.* (First Series), vol. vii. p. 172.
[2] *Op. cit.*, p. 164.

PLATE XVII.

THE BRUGH OF THE BOYNE, NEW GRANGE, COUNTY MEATH.

PLATE XVIII.

DOORWAY OF THE BRUGH OF THE BOYNE.

PLATE XIX.

GROUND PLAN OF THE BRUGH OF THE BOYNE

(as at present explored).

PLATES XVII., XVIII., AND XIX.—*Brugh of the Boyne,*
New Grange, County Meath.

The diagrams here shown are from drawings by Mr. W. F.
Wakeman, the veteran Irish archæologist.[1] With reference to
the spiral carvings at the doorway of the Brugh, it may be
mentioned that " the same kind of ornament appears on a stone
found amidst a heap which had once been a ' Pict's-house ' in
the island of Eday, Orkney ; "[2] and that in Orkney, also, there
has been found, in an underground house, a large stone
"saucer," or "tray," resembling the two shown in the ground
plan of the Brugh. (There appears to be no settled opinion
as to the uses of those " saucers.")

In connection with the identification of this mound with the
" Brugh of the Boyne " of ancient Irish history, the following
remarks may be quoted. The Rev. Father O'Laverty, in the
Journal of the Royal Society of Antiquaries of Ireland
(December, 1892, p. 430) thus observes :—

---

[1] Earlier illustrations, from drawings made in 1724 by Mr. Samuel
Molyneux, a Dublin student, may be seen in Part II. of " A Natural
History of Ireland," Dublin, 1726. Other eighteenth-century repre-
sentations of the same place occur in a volume of old plates, belonging
to the Society of Antiquaries (London). This volume is endorsed
" Celtic Remains ; I," and its contents form part of (says the fly-leaf)
" a collection of plates from the Archæologia collected by Mr. Akerman
when the Society's Stock was sold off and arranged more or less in
Classes." The views of the Brugh will be found at pp. 239, 253, and
254 (Plates XIX.-XXII.). Colonel Forbes Leslie has two excellent
plates, from drawings of his own, in his *Early Races of Scotland* (Edin.
1866), vol. ii. ; where he also refers to Wilde's *Boyne and Blackwater*
and Wakeman's *Irish Antiquities.* A recent work, illustrating the same
subject, but which I have not yet had an opportunity of seeing, is Mr.
George Coffey's " Tumuli and Inscribed Stones at New Grange, Dowth,
and Knowth," Dublin, 1893.

[2] Forbes Leslie's *Early Races of Scotland,* vol. ii. p. 335, *note.*

" In his very valuable work, *The Boyne and Blackwater*, Sir
William Wilde appears to me to have used convincing arguments
to prove that *Brugh-na-Boinne* . . . . was . . . . on the left bank
of the Boyne, convenient to the ford of *Ros-na-righ* (Rossnaree) at
Knowth, Dowth, and Newgrange. To Sir William's arguments
one point only was wanting : the old name had disappeared. . . . .
It is now more than thirty years since I went to Newgrange for
the special purpose of investigating that matter. I explained to
Mr. Maguire, then of Newgrange, and to his son, that *Brugh-no-
Boinne* signified ' the town, or dwelling-place, on the Boyne,' that
the word *Brugh* would assume the modern form *Bro*, as in
Brughshane (pronounced Broshane), and many other townland
names, and that *na-Boinne*, ' of the Boyne,' would probably cease
to be used as unnecessary at the site. I need not say that I was
greatly pleased when they informed me that the field in which is
the mound of Newgrange is called the *Bro-Park*, while in the
immediate vicinity are the *Bro-Farm*, the *Bro-Mill*, and the *Bro-
Cottage*." [And also, they might have added, the mansion of
Broe House.]

Any one, therefore, who duly considers the matter, in relation
to the statements of both of these writers, will see that the
mound at New Grange is the *Brugh-na-Boinne* of Irish history
and tradition. And this name, says Father O'Laverty,
"signified ' the town, or dwelling-place, on the Boyne.' " What,
then, are the earliest associations with this "town or dwelling-
place ? "

It is said [1] to have been built by a celebrated "king and
oracle" of the people known as the Tuatha Dé, Dea, or De
Danann, and to have been the residence of himself and others
of his race. This chief (Eochaid *Ollathair*) is usually referred
to as "the Dagda," or "the Daghda Mòr"; and of his nation
it is asserted that, after having invaded Ireland and conquered

---

[1] O'Curry's *Lectures*, Dublin, 1861, p. 505.

its native "Fir-Bolgs," they were themselves conquered in turn by a later race of immigrants, the Gaels. This "Brugh," therefore, is said to have been the residence of the Dagda, and, after him, of Angus, one of his sons. Consequently, it is very frequently styled "the Brugh of Angus, son of the Dagda," an appellation which assumes various forms.[1] Latterly, it seems to have been most generally known as "the Brugh" (*par excellence*), or, more simply still, as "Brugh." In the Book of Leinster it is specified as one of "Ireland's three undeniable eminences [*dindgna*]"[2]; while "an ancient poem by Mac Nia, son of Oenna (in the Book of Ballymote, fol. 190 b.)," styles it "a king's mansion" and a "*sidh*." The same MS. (32 *a b*) gives the variant *Sidh an Bhrogha*, rendered by Dr. Standish O'Grady "the fairy fort of the *Brugh* upon the Boyne."[3] This word "*sidh*," which was applied—probably in the first place—to hollow mounds such as this, but which was also applied to the dwellers in them, gave the Tuatha De Danann their most popular name. Because it was on account of their residence in "the green mounds, known by the name of *Sidh*," that they were called "the *Fir Sidhe* [*i.e.*, men of the *sidhs*], or Fairies, of Ireland."[4] The one word, indeed (*sidh*), became indifferently applied to the dwellings and the dwellers. Whichever was the earliest meaning of that word, there is little dubiety as to the etymology of *Siabhra*. In one copy of the *Leabhar na h-Uidhre*,[5] it is stated that the Tuatha De Danann

---

[1] For most of which see Dr. Standish O'Grady's *Silva Gadelica*, pp. 102-3, 146, 233, 474, and 484.

[2] *Silva Gadelica* (English translation), pp. 474 and 520.

[3] *Op. cit.* (English translation), p. 522.

[4] Skene's *Celtic Scotland*, vol. iii. pp. 106-7.

[5] Class H. 3, 17, Trinity College, Dublin. [I quote from Mr. Petrie's "Round Towers," Trans. of Roy. Irish Acad., vol. xx. (Dublin, 1845), p. 90.]

E

"were called *Siabhras.*" O'Reilly defines *siabhra* as "a fairy," and *siabhrach* as "fairy-like"; while "a fairy mansion" is *siabhrugh.* With Connellan, again, *siabhrog* is "a fairy." It seems quite evident that these are all corruptions of *sidh-bhrugh* (otherwise *Sidh an Bhrogha,* as above), and that *Siabhra,* as applied to the *dwellers,* was simply a transference from the name denoting their *dwellings.*

Numerous as are the references to this mound as a "dwelling-place," its name figures prominently in the list of the ancient cemeteries of Ireland. *Relec in Broga,* "the Cemetery of the Brugh," is referred to as one of "the three cemeteries of Idolaters," in an Irish manuscript of the twelfth century (or earlier), the *Leabhar na h-Uidhre* cited above. Of the two others, one is "the Cemetery of Cruachan"; and, by glancing at it, in the first place, we shall obtain a good idea of the Cemetery of the Brugh. "We find that the monuments within the cemetery at Rathcroghan,"[1] says Mr. Petrie, "are small circular mounds, which, when examined, are found to cover rude, sepulchral chambers formed of stone, without cement of any kind, and containing unburned bones."[2] And the twelfth-century scribe whom Mr. Petrie largely quotes, says that there were fifty such mounds (*cnoc*) in the cemetery at Cruachan. This mediæval scholar has copied a poem on the subject, "ascribed to Dorban, a poet of West Connaught," wherein it is said that it is not in the power of poets or of sages to reckon the number of heroes under the Cruachan mounds, and that there is not a hillock (*cnoc*) in that cemetery "which is not the grave of a king or royal prince, or of a woman, or warlike poet."

---

[1] Rath Chruachain, Co. Roscommon: the cemetery was styled *Relig na Riogh,* or the Cemetery of Kings.

[2] *Op cit,,* p. 106.

In another verse, he says that *each* of the fifty mounds had a warrior under it; and, altogether, it appears that, although their number could doubtless be "reckoned," yet the burial mounds of Cruachan, in or about the twelfth century, much exceeded fifty in number. "Fifty" is simply used by the poet and his commentator to show that, like the two other cemeteries of the triad (each of which is also said to have had fifty) the Cemetery of Cruachan contained about a third of the pagan notables of Ireland.

From this we see that, about the twelfth century, the Cemetery of the Brugh contained at least fifty sepulchral mounds such as those described by Mr. Petrie at Cruachan. Mr. Petrie further quotes two passages from the *Dinnsenchus*, which specify in the following terms some of the most famous of those "monuments" at the Brugh :—

"The Grave [or Stone Cairn, *Leacht*] of the Dagda ; the Grave of Aedh Luirgnech, son of the Dagda ; the Graves of Cirr and Cuirrell, wives of the Dagda—'these are two hillocks [*da cnoc*]' ; the Grave of Esclam, the Dagda's Brehon, ' which is called *Fert-Patric* at this day' ; the Cashel [or Stone Enclosure] of Angus, son of Crunmael; the Cave [*Derc*] of Buailcc Bec ; the Stone Cairn [*Leacht*] of Cellach, son of Maelcobha ; the Stone Cairn [*Leacht*] of the steed of Cinaedh, son of Irgalach; the Prison [*Carcar*] of Liath-Macha ; the 'Glen' of the Mata ; the Pillar Stone of Buidi, the son of Muiredh, where his head is interred ; the Stone of Benn; the Grave of Boinn, the wife of Nechtan ; the 'Bed' of the daughter of Forann ; the *Barc* of Crimthann Nianar, in which he was interred ; the Grave of Fedelmidh, the Lawgiver ; the *Cumot* of Cairbre Lifeachair ; the *Fulacht* of Fiachna Sraiphtine."

These, of course, are only some of the most famous of the sepulchral monuments which existed in the Cemetery of the

Brugh eight or nine centuries ago. Since that time, most of
them have disappeared, their stones having been presumably
built into castles, mansions, cottages and walls, while the
bones of the queens and heroes have fertilised the soil of the
neighbouring farms. But there still remain a few "standing-
stones" and "moats" in the vicinity of the Brugh, all of
which may be included in the above list.

I have cited that list for the reason that modern antiquaries,
or many of them, have assumed that *Sid in Broga* and *Relec in
Broga* are synonymous terms, and that when a king or hero
is recorded to have been buried "at Brugh," that means that
he was buried *in* the Brugh itself. In other words, that a
place which was known as Fert-Patrick in or about the twelfth
century, as also the "cashel" and the many hillocks, graves,
and cairns mentioned in the list—not to speak of innumerable
others—were all situated in the chamber which is shown in
Plate XIX. It does not require a moment's reflection to con-
vince one that this is an erroneous assumption. Nor is it
warranted by the "History of the Cemeteries" itself, which
always speaks of the burials having been "*at* Brugh."[1]

One other statement, however, must be referred to. In
another verse of Dorban's poem, mentioned above, it is said
that "the host of Meath" are buried "*ar lár in Broga tuathaig.*"
This is rendered by Petrie, "in the middle of the lordly Brugh."
The translation is no doubt good; and it is open to any one to

---

[1] "*Is in Brug,* or *Bruig.*" Mr. Petrie invariably translates this as
"at" Brugh. But I observe that Dr. Standish O'Grady (*Silva Gadelica,*
p. 256 ; and p. 289 of English translation) renders the Gaelic particle
by English "in." To decide between two Gaelic scholars is not within
my province. But if Dr. O'Grady understands "the Brugh" to be
synonymous with *Sidh an Bhrogha* (as perhaps he does not), the adoption
of his reading would lead to an inference which is opposed to common
sense.

deduce therefrom that the chamber shown in the plan contained at one time the skeletons of the host of Meath. In that case, the "host" must have been very limited in number; and any one who has crawled along the sixty-foot passage into the Brugh, and who adopts this view, must wonder a little as to how the corpses were conveyed along that passage, and as to the reasons which must have induced some people (prior to 1699, when the chamber was almost, if not altogether, void of such relics)[1] to drag all those bones out again, at much personal inconvenience. But "*ar lár in Broga*" may also mean "in the [burying-] ground of the Brugh"; and the descriptions quoted above from the *Dinnsenchus* show quite clearly that the ground in which "the host of Meath" were buried embraced a considerable tract of land, dotted over with mounds and monuments, differing only in degree from those of a modern cemetery.[2]

The twelfth-century commentator of Dorban's poem states:

"The nobles of the Tuatha De Danann (with the exception of seven of them who were interred at Talten [which was the third 'Cemetery of the Idolaters']) were buried at Brugh, *i.e.*, Lugh, and Oe, son of Ollamh, and Ogma, and Carpre, son of Etan, and Etan (the poetess) herself, and the Dagda and his three sons (*i.e.*, Aedh, and Oengus, and Cermait), and a great

---

[1] Molyneux, writing in 1725, says that "when first the cave was opened, the bones of two dead bodies entire, not burnt, were found upon the floor." Colonel Forbes Leslie remarks: "Llhuyd, the antiquary, writing in 1699, makes no mention of any human remains being found in it."

[2] Since the above was written, the quarterly number, June 1893, of the *Journal of the Royal Society of Antiquaries of Ireland* has been issued, and a note therein confirms the suspicion, indicated in Mr. Wakeman's drawing, that the whole mound is not yet explored. But the above remarks are applicable in any case.

many others besides of the Tuatha De Dananns, and Firbolgs and others."[1]

But, afterwards, "the race of Heremon, *i.e.*, the kings of Tara," who used to bury at Cruachan (because that was the chief seat in their special principality of Connaught) came to bury at Brugh. "The first king of them that was interred at Brugh" was a certain Crimthann, surnamed *Nianar*, the son of Lughaidh Riabh-n-derg ; and the reason why Crimthann decided to abandon the burying-place of his forefathers was " because his wife Nar was of the Tuatha Dea, and it was she solicited him that he should adopt Brugh as a burial-place for himself and his descendants, and this was the cause that they did not bury at Cruachan."[3] It would appear that the ruling dynasty of the Tuatha Dea had ended in a female, both on account of Nar's action in this matter, and because her husband became known by her name—as Nianar (*Niadh-Náir*) or " Nar's Champion."

This Nar is a very interesting personage in the present connection. Because, being one of the Tuatha Dea, she was a *siabhra*, or woman of the *sidhs ;* otherwise, a *bean-síde* (modernised into "banshee"). This is plainly stated in two other Irish manuscripts, with an additional explanation which is very apposite. It is said that Crimthann was called Nar's Champion "because his wife Nar *thuathchaech* out of the *sidhes*, or of the Pict-folk [*a sídaib no do Chruithentuaith*], she it was that took him off on an adventure." A companion statement is that made in another manuscript to the effect

[1] Petrie : *op. cit.*, p. 106.

[3] That is, Lughaidh of the Red Stripes ; "meaning that on his person he had two such : one as girdle round his middle, another as necklace round his neck." (*Silva Gadelica*, English translation, p. 544.)

[3] Petrie (*op. cit.*, p. 101), quoting from the " History of the Cemeteries " in the *Leabhar na h-Uidhre.*

Durchschnitt des Denghoog 1/100 nat Größe

Grundriss 1/250 nat. Größe   a. Feuerstätte.   S. Denghoog.

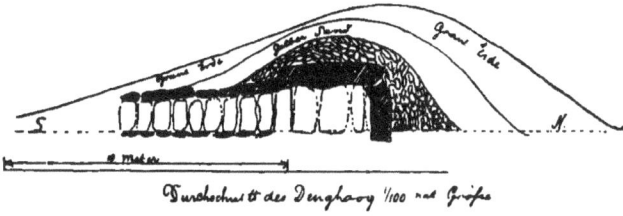

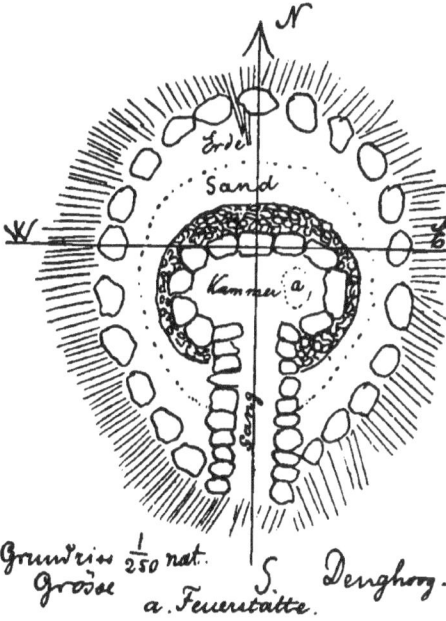

SECTIONAL VIEW AND GROUND PLAN OF THE DENGHOOG,
ISLAND OF SYLT.

that " Nar *thuathchaech*, the daughter of Lotan of the Pict-folk [*Nár thuathchaech ingen Lotain do Chruithentuaith*], was the mother of Feradach *finnfhechtnach*," or " the brightly prosperous "—a king of Ireland.[1]

Incidentally, therefore, in considering the Brugh of the Boyne and the people most associated with it, we find very distinct confirmation of the main part of the contention in the foregoing treatise. From these extracts it is evident that those early writers regarded *siabhra, fear-sidh, bean-sidh*, and *daoine-sidh* (words which may also be interpreted " mound-dweller ") as ordinary folk-names for the Picts ; just in the same way as any historian of the frontier wars in North America would understand by " Red-skin " and " Greaser " the more classic " Indian " and " Mexican."

PLATES XX. AND XXI.—*The Denghoog, Island of Sylt, North Friesland.*

In addition to my original collection, I am now able to show three views of the Denghoog, in Sylt, which is the mound referred to on p. 34 (*ante*). Mr. W. G. Black speaks of it thus :—

"There is some confusion as to King Finn's dwelling. As doctors differ, we may be allowed to claim that it was the Denghoog, close to Wenningstedt, if only because we descended into that remarkable dwelling. Externally merely a swelling green mound, like so many others in Sylt, entrance is gained by a trap-door in the roof, and decending a steep ladder, one finds himself in a subterranean chamber, some seventeen by ten feet in size, the walls of which are twelve huge blocks of Swedish granite ;

---

[1] These two extracts are from *Silva Gadelica*, Eng. transl., pp. 495 and 544 ; where the references are, respectively, "Book of Ballymote, 250 a b," and " Kilbride No. 3, Advocates' Library, Edinburgh, 5."

the height of the roof varies from five feet to six feet. The original entrance appears to have been a long narrow passage, seventeen feet long and about two feet wide and high. This mound was examined by a Hamburg professor in 1868, who found remains of a fireplace, bones of a small man, some clay urns, and stone weapons. Later, a Kiel professor is said to have carried off all he found therein to Kiel Museum, and so far we have not been able to trace the published accounts of his investigations."[1]

Mr. Christian Jensen, Oevenum, Föhr, to whom I am indebted for these three views, has favoured me with the following information :—

" The sketches of the Denhoog which I enclose [viz., the Ground Plan and Sectional View] are from the drawings of Professor Wibel, who conducted the excavation of it in 1868. From his and C. P. Hansen's observations I contribute the following statements : Originally, the mound was higher, but in 1868 it had the form of a truncated cone, 4½ *mètres* [say 14 feet 9 inches] in height. As may be seen from the picture, it slopes away to the south above the original passage into the mound, which the dweller made use of as his entrance ; so that the extent is very considerable. The present entrance, as may be seen from the view of the interior, was made from above, at the north side, directly opposite the original entrance. . . . . Dr. Wibel says : ' At the south side of the chamber is the doorway for ingress and egress, with the passage itself leading from it. This passage, which was 6 *mètres* [19 feet 8 inches] in length, was lined with upright blocks of granite and gneiss, with a roofing and floor made of flagstones of the same kinds of stone. It was opened up all the way to the mouth of the passage. This [the outer orifice] lay close to the extremity of the earth and near the floor of the mound, was closed with earth only, not with a stone, and measured about 1 *mètre* [3 feet 3.4 inches] in height, and 1½ *mètre* in breadth. On account of these dimensions . . . . one

---

[1] *Heligoland*, Edin. and Lond., 1888, pp. 84-85.

PLATE XXII.

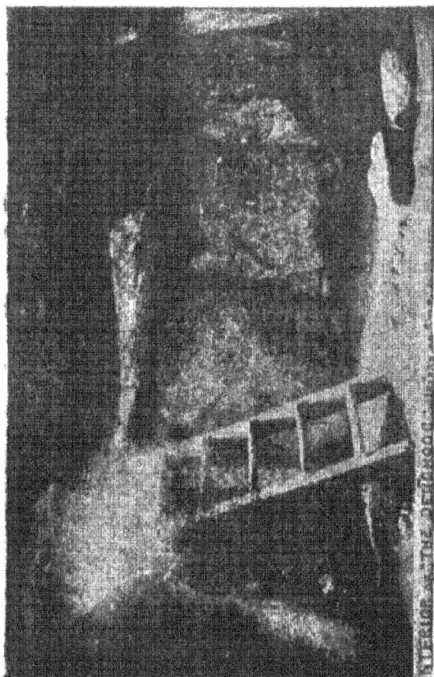

INTERIOR OF THE DENGHOOG, ISLAND OF SYLT.

can only creep through with difficulty, and for that reason the plan does not show with accuracy the position of the wall-slabs, and their number is merely conjectured to be nine.'

" Immediately after this excavation of 17–19 September, 1868, C. P. Hansen writes as follows:—

" 'There are in the island of Sylt hillocks of ancient origin, for the most part pagan burying-places, but some of which may have served as the dwelling-places of a primitive people. One such hillock has just been opened at Wenningstedt. The interior was found to be a chamber, 17 feet long, 10 feet in breadth, and from 5 to 6 feet in height, with a covered passage about 22 feet long, trending southward. The walls of this underground room were composed of twelve large granite blocks, regularly arranged ; the roof consisted of three still larger slabs of the same kind of rock ; the stones which formed the passage were smaller. At one corner of the floor of the cellar there was a well-defined fireplace, and near it were urns and flint implements ; in the opposite corner there were many bones lying, apparently unburned, probably those of the last dweller in the cavern.' "

Mr. Christian Jensen gives an account of " Der Denghoog bei Wenningstedt " in the " Beilage zu Nr. 146 der Flensburger Nachrichten " of 25th June 1893, in which he says :

" . . . . On the floor of the chamber, three separate divisions were distinctly visible, of which one, situated on the east side, showed traces of having been a fireplace. Professor Wibel found several fragments of human bones, which evidently belonged only to *one* individual, as no portion was duplicated ; also a few animals' bones. There was an extraordinary number of fragments of pottery, belonging to about 24 different urns, of which 11 could be put together. Their form and ornamentation were both fine and varied, an interesting witness to the ceramics of the grey past. . . . Among the stone implements found were a great many flint-knives ; two stone hatchets, two chisels, and a gouge, all of flint, and a disc of porphyry were also obtained. Several mineral substances, quartzite, rubble-stones, gravel, ochre, a sinter-heap —these are less interesting than the seven amber beads which, with some charcoal, completes the list of objects found. Referring to former investigations of galleried mounds [*gangbauten*], which seem to have been used in some cases as burying-places, in others as dwellings, Dr. Wibel observes, in answer to the question resulting from his discovery, as to whether the Denghoog ought to be regarded as a sepulchre or as a dwelling, that, as Nilsson has already said, all gallery-mounds were originally dwellings, and occasionally became utilised as tombs. In the case of the Denghoog, this fact is demonstrated by the fireplace, the scattered potsherds, the amber beads, &c."

Of the little woodcut which forms the Tailpiece of this volume, it is hardly necessary to say that it represents some popular ideas regarding "the little people." The woodcut of which this is a facsimile is one of those contained in the eighteenth-century chap-book, "*Round about our Coal Fire;* or, Christmas Entertainments," and it heads the chapter "*Of Fairies, their Use and Dignity.*" "They generally came out of a Mole-hill," it is said; "they had fine Musick always among themselves, and Danced in a Moonshiny Night around, or in a Ring as one may see at this Day upon every Common in *England*, where Mushroones [*sic*] grow." The size of the mushroom, so elegantly depicted in the foreground, is quite on a scale suitable to the stature ultimately accorded to the little people in many districts; so also is the mole-hill. But the tree, and the Satanic head in the foliage, are curiously out of proportion.

An examination of these various diagrams will show that the more primitive of those structures were obviously built by a small-sized race; some of the passages being quite impassable to large men of the present day. This peculiarity was noticed by Scott when visiting the "brochs" of Shetland, a kindred class of structures (none of which are here shown). "These Duns or Picts' Castles are so small," he says, writing in his Diary in August 1814, "it is impossible to conceive what effectual purpose they could serve excepting a temporary refuge for the chief." This reflection was suggested to him by the Broch of Cleik-him-in (now usually written Clickemin), near Lerwick; and in describing it he says: "The interior gallery, with its apertures, is so extremely low and narrow, being only about three feet square, that it is difficult to conceive how it could serve the purpose of communication. At any rate, the size fully justifies the tradition prevalent here, as well as in the south of Scotland, that the Picts were a diminutive race." Of the Broch of Mousa he says: "The uppermost gallery is so narrow and low that it was with great difficulty I crept through it,"—a feat which baffled the present writer.[1] In all those cases, of course, it is understood one has to crawl. As with the Lapps and the Eskimos, creeping was much more a matter of course with the builders of those places than it is with us. After getting through such passages it happens that, in several instances, the roof is higher than is required for the tallest living man.

---

[1] On the very topmost course of all, the gallery dwindles into such insignificant dimensions that not even a dwarf (as one would naturally understand that term) could creep along it. Scott cannot have meant this very extremity. With regard to it, I should be inclined to say that it was merely the necessary finish of the gallery, not intended to be used any more than the spaces beside the eaves of a house.

An admirable example of such a place is the underground
" Picts' House " at Pitcur, in Forfarshire, which would be
quite a palace to people of a small race, and very likely figures
as such in some popular tale ; its dimensions and appearance
considerably magnified with every century.[1] But even this
" fairy palace " was entered by narrow, downward-sloping
passages, similar to that seen in the Frontispiece, down and up
which the dwellers had to crawl. An underground gallery
such as that of Ardtole (near Ardglass, County Down), is
somewhat puzzling, because, while one chamber off it rises to
a height of 5 feet 3 inches, another is only 3½ feet high; and
the main gallery, for 70 feet of its length, is 4½ feet high, with
a width of 3 feet 4 inches. The inference from this seems to
be that the occupants were under 4½ feet in height. If they
had intended to crawl along the 70 feet, they did not require
so high a roof; whereas, if they walked, and if they were more
than 4½ feet in height, they would need to walk the 70 feet in
a stooping posture, a constraint which they could easily have
avoided by raising the roof a foot or two. The highest roof
in all this souterrain being 5 feet 3, it does not seem likely
that the builders were taller than that ; and there seems more
reason to believe that they were much smaller. Another such
gallery in Sutherlandshire is "nowhere more than 4½ feet in
height, and for the greater part of its length only 2 feet wide,
expanding to 3½, for about 3 feet only from the inner end."
Still more restricted is the "rath-cave" of Ballyknock, in the
parish of Ballynoe, barony of Kinnatalloon, County Cork.
"The cave is a mere cutting in the clayey subsoil, and is

---

[1] The tendency to " idealisation on the part of the narrator " is referred
to, in this connection, by Mr. Joseph Jacobs, at p. 242 of his " English
Fairy Tales " (London, D. Nutt, 1890).

roofed with flags resting on the clayey banks of the cutting, of which the length is about 100 feet, and the height and width from 3 to 3½ feet, except that the width to a height of 2 feet is hardly a foot at the N.W. turn, 23 feet from the N.E. end, and at a point 27 feet from the S.E. end. . . . . Right below the aperture . . . . was a short pillar-stone, deeply scored with Oghams . . . . [and] many of the roofing slabs were seen . . . . to be inscribed with Oghams, some large and others minute." [1]

" This class of structures deserves a careful study," observes Captain Thomas, referring to the souterrains of the north-west of Scotland; [2] "for the room or accommodation afforded by this mode of building is exceedingly small when compared with the labour expended in procuring it; besides, the doorway · or entry is often so contracted that no bulky object, not even a very stout man, could get in. . . . . But what are we to think when the single passage is so small that only a child could crawl through it ? "

---

[1] *Jour. Roy. Soc. Antiq. Ireland*, 1891 (Third Quarter), p. 517. It is not inappropriate to add that one of these inscriptions reads : " Branan, son of Ochal," and that the decipherer (the Rev. Edmond Barry, M.R.I.A.) identifies this latter name with "the name of a King of the Fairies of Connaught (*Ri Side Connacht*) " : *op. cit.*, pp. 524–525. The Ardtole souterrain is described in the Journal of the same Society (July–October, 1889, p. 245), by Mr. Seaton F. Milligan, M.R.I.A. ; and the one in Sutherlandshire is referred to by Dr. Joseph Anderson (at p. 289 of " Scotland in Pagan Times : The Iron Age," Edinburgh, 1883).

[2] *Proc. Soc. Antiq. Scot.* (First Series), vol. vii. pp. 185–6.